Times Like These

Michelle Langstone

Times Like These

On grief, hope & remarkable love

First published in 2021

Allen & Unwin
Level 2, 10 College Hill, Freemans Bay
Auckland 1011, New Zealand
Phone: (64 9) 377 3800
Email: auckland@allenandunwin.com
Web: www.allenandunwin.co.nz

83 Alexander Street
Crows Nest NSW 2065, Australia
Phone: (61 2) 8425 0100

A catalogue record for this book is available from the National Library of New Zealand.

ISBN 978 1 98854 752 7

Design by Megan van Staden
Set in Fairfield LH 12/18
Printed and bound in Australia by Griffin Press, part of Ovato

10 9 8 7 6 5 4 3 2 1

For my family

Contents

Parade

I held my father close as he left us and I didn't let go. His death interrupted the processional sun of an ordinary morning, and it kept us back from the rest of the world beyond the room where he lay. Everything flowing on like a river, like a ribbon, like a tide around us while we took the last molecules of breath he had let go of, and pressed them to our eyelids and our cheeks. I kissed him. I was not afraid of his gone skin, of his gone eyes, and the set of his gone jaw. I kissed the cliff of his cheekbones and the gully below them, where freckles I had counted like constellations in recent weeks seemed to disappear with the colour that fled his cheeks.

I unwrapped my hand from his and felt coolness reach the space where he had been. I pressed the pads of his fingers against my own. We spread like starfish, and

I wanted to push his nails in, to leave waning moons in my flesh to keep him close. Instead I felt their trimmed sharpness and cried, because I had cut them only yesterday, when he was very alive, and my mother had asked why I was holding the scissors that way. It had taken me thirty-nine years and his imminent death to learn the sharp sickle of the blades should face inward and follow the curve of your nails when you cut them. That's what I thought of in the minutes after he died.

We knew Dad was dying; we were prepared and we understood. We had dwindled toward this point over many, many months, and yet the complete absence of him in an instant was staggering. I lay my head on his chest, and there was nothing where for months I had charted a faint gurgling of a blocked drain in the centre of him and I had listened to his strong heart holding steady in spite of it, or because of it, anchoring him to the firmament as a barnacle clings to a boat. Those sounds—the coughs, the sleep-moaning, the rattling in the dark—were the soundtrack of our lives for months, and now the record had been changed and I was not ready.

That he was recalcitrant at the time of departure should not have surprised me. I've never met a human being more stubbornly determined to be in the world. There was no man more full of the joy of living than my father. There was no man more reluctant to part with it. Our doctor came into the room on a day where things had got very bad, and he must have seen the desperation in our eyes; we didn't understand how it could take Dad so long to leave us when his body was so broken. 'Why would you want to leave when there is so much love in the room,' the doctor said, and I looked at Dad, fast asleep at that point, and thought—You sneak. You've got us right where you want us, all in the room for days on end, sleeping beside you, brushing our teeth at the foot of your bed, arguing over the remote and getting crumbs on the coverlet. For his passing we had created the dream of his life: all of us together, keeping watch over his parade at the end of the world.

The first text message Dad ever sent to me was about how he thought it would be tip top to have a family lunch on Sunday, like the old days. He'd held out for years after the technology breakthrough, stubborn, refusing to buy a cellphone, but had finally given in, such were his feelings about lunch. He signed off on the text *From Dad*, as if I didn't know who it would be sending it. I registered all requirements in an instant, because he had made an institution of Sunday lunch before I knew how to read. Sunday lunch around the wooden table I'd carved my initials into with a fork tine, and been thumped for in punishment, age eight. Sunday lunch where we first saw the signs of Alzheimer's in my nana, who used her table knife to gouge huge slippery chunks of margarine from the pottle and lop them on a slice of salami to eat. Sunday lunch, no singing at the table. Sunday lunch carefully parting leaves of iceberg lettuce from the stem to make cups for tomato and cucumber with malt vinegar and cheese. Sunday lunch evolving alongside the bread industry, first white, then wholemeal loaves; rolls with cheese on them when the supermarket got a fancy bread section; branching out into sticks of French origin, deepening into rye loaves from the new bakery up the street—sourdough and things with seeds more lately. In the months before his death he came back around to white bread. It was security for his insides that had forgotten what to do with food, and security for his heart, which needed comfort and knowable things in the face of death.

Lunch was more to Dad than food. It was all his humans gathered close together where he could look at us, and laugh with us, and yell if necessary. It was this tradition that built the structure of our world, and love laid out as a tablecloth that bound us. Here is the story of a family of five, recorded in sandwiches and cups of cordial and, later, cool glasses of shandy and foamy beer. 'Tip top, Mouse,' he'd say to me. 'Tip top.'

We argued about why nobody had thought to bring massage cream for Dad's legs. Irritable, scratched like panes of glass, we bickered. Dad frowned at us, rolling his head side to side across the pillow to take us in. 'Don't argue,' he mouthed, rasps of voice meeting the air. In the end I found hand cream in Mum's bag and used that to try to distract him from how hard it was to breathe. His ragged breaths, our ragged hearts, a plastic tube of hand cream that smelled of freesias and an unreachable springtime. Scars ran the side of one foot like a map for treasure. There were metal plates and screws I could feel with my fingertips, his skin was so thin. For a time we were quiet, then Dad had had enough and he motioned me away. I laid the sheets across him, and I adjusted the fan to blow on him because the movement of air made him feel he was breathing better. Dad raised his eyebrows at me, waggled them half-heartedly, and tried to smile.

On the stairs in our entranceway you could perch and feel the measure of the whole house. The staircase ran down through the centre in five levels, with thick wooden bannisters we learned to balance on, terrifying our mother, daring each other to scale down into the dark, down to the rumpus room with the concrete walls. I sat on the stairs that faced the front door on the day Dad turned forty, and I watched the streams of strangers come into our home. In fancy dress I didn't recognise anyone; people waved at me, men in suits and wigs gave me the thumbs-up, and the volume rose. Dad darted in and out of company, bent at the waist, an unlit cigar in his mouth, puffing ostentatiously and grinning like a maniac. His thick inky eyebrows and moustache stayed fixed, and I pressed my thumb and forefinger together and felt the residue of spirit gum there from when he'd shown me how to do it. The gum had smelt like the rosin I used on my violin strings, and he'd painted it carefully onto the fluffy black material with a tiny brush. I helped press it above his top lip and onto his eyebrows, which he waggled, making me laugh. He added glasses, attached to which was a plastic nose. Tailcoat, white shirt, bow tie, shiny black shoes, and pants my mum had pressed for him. Away he went as Groucho Marx, and he stayed in character all night. He never dropped his role. Even when I begged him to just be my dad and say goodnight as I was trundling off to bed, he wouldn't budge. I lay in my room lit softly by the outside light and wondered if he would ever come back.

In the pale room we camped around him, four weary, frightened monuments to love. It felt grotesque in a way, to preside over his death, but what else could you do for a giant made so small by disease. We grew larger in spirit, filling the room to block up any holes he might slip through when we weren't watching. The dusk before he died I stayed beside him while the others went home for a few hours to feed the cats and pretend to be normal. He was fitful, in and out of dark clouds of difficulty, a low-pressure system hovering, turning his lungs into storm drains. I turned the cricket on for comfort, but the light hurt his eyes. I turned off all the lights and it was too dark for him. I turned on a lamp and I climbed into my little bed in the corner and lay on my side facing him, and we talked. I hoped he would fall asleep as night drew close. I told him again and again to lay his head down and rest. Later I thought about how daft that was. Those were his last days with us, what did sleep matter? What were we resting him for?

As he gave over his autonomy to the infection deep inside, he began to hallucinate. I dozed and woke abruptly many times, a light flickering on and off, and each time I came round there was a new idea. 'I'll tell you what we'll do, Mouse, we'll rob a bank. That's what we're going to do, you and me. Don't tell your mother.' We ran over the plans for a smooth bank heist to make sure the family had enough money after he was gone. I was to be the distraction—I'd do all the yelling out front, and Dad would bring his tool kit; he was sure there'd be something in there to help with the safe. He asked where we kept the balaclavas and I told him they were in my bag. He asked me how many banks I had robbed and I told him eleven. We did sums again and again, checking and double-checking how far things could stretch. 'A million should be all right,' he said. 'You should be all right with that.' He was so worried about what he was leaving behind.

Dad grew up in a house with a solo mother and five older brothers, including a set of twins. Money was stretched tight, a glove too small for a hand. Dad had a paper round, and delivered parcels for the Post Office to earn money. He took home damaged goods to share—stiff cardboard boxes of broken sampler biscuits. Six boys in a house they'd built for their mum, a woman who worked every hour of daylight and many shifts through the dark to keep them clothed. Six boys without much of a dad to go on, raising themselves in the image of what they imagined a loving man could be. A Loving Man went to work for his family. A Loving Man opened the door in the evening and called out to his boys, who ran to him. A Loving Man taught them how to hammer nails and ride bikes and run fast.

Dad went on a road trip to Rotorua with his father—an unexpected delight, a wonder. I imagine him there on the car ride, his head out the window like a puppy, breathing the travelling air and grinning for this moment with his Loving Man. He was locked in a motel unit for the better part of an afternoon, and all night, while his dad went gambling. The money was lost, and they drove home in a volatile fug of cigarette smoke and alcohol sweat. Dad never saw his father again. He was six years old.

I called my family just before midnight. It was the call we had feared, its shadow looming over us all week and crouching in the corner with terrible patience. We took our places, and all through that night we rode the storm. Rough waves of terror as the breathing became impossible, soft lulls as the panic abated and the drugs calmed the swell. When morning came we drew back the curtains and the room flooded with early sun, and it fell on the white coverlet and it fell on our hands that were holding his. Eyes shut tight and jaw set with the grimace of endurance, Dad eased his head toward the window and sunlight met his forehead like a blessing. The Eagles sang 'Take It Easy' to him over my little speaker. He tilted his face and the sunlight found his mouth, and the etching of a seventy-two-year-old smile revealed itself.

In the little cove the tide was full. We kids took turns to dive off the bow of the boat, swimming deep to touch the anchor, shouting in victory as our heads broke the surface. The boat swung gently on the chain, so the radio reached us in swells of song just long enough to hear the chorus before it ebbed away again. Dad sat on the duckboard in faded lime-green shorts, his feet in the water, a beer in his hand. He'd knock back his head to look at the sky and let the sun hit his face, or he'd run his hand along the trim of the stern and feel the whorls of wood beneath his fingers.

The song on the radio changed and he made a sound of approval, bobbing his head to the beat. He turned to look at us, sleek otters rolling in the blue sea, and called out across the water. 'This is the life, eh!'

This is the life.

Wet Season

We began our grieving before Dad left us. We had time to imagine our lives without him, and into that future we filed our sadness and our loss, and let it hang there, a portrait of a lesser-numbered family with an empty space where he had been. We made deals with his painful, slow decline; somewhere inside ourselves we wrote contracts that witnessing his death in such close colour, holding him across eighteen months as he made preparations to leave us, meant we would recover more quickly on the other side. Like astronauts who had lost one of the team on an expedition and come back to Earth broken but otherwise unharmed, we had done the work and felt the sadness and the loss each day for our man, and for this courage we would be rewarded and the grief would be easier to bear. It's incredible how wrong you can be. One year after his passing, I still wake in the morning with a forgotten mind, then as I register the light through the curtains and the quality of the day I remember he is gone, and this knowledge comes like a sickening plummet on a ride I can't get off and never had a ticket for. It is the same for everyone in my family. Our grief moves with the kinetic energy of dominoes; we fall one after the other, collapse in a heaped pattern of loss, and then reassemble.

Dad's funeral felt almost euphoric, and it tricked me. We were so full of love for him, and for his life, and for the people who had come to remember him that it felt we would be carried aloft with the celebration of him forever. It was expansive, like the air you draw into your lungs in a deep, cool forest. It was the lungfuls of sweet air we took for him and his tired lungs that had just left us. It was wonderful and sad, that funeral. It was radiant with the spirit of our funny man, and when it came time to carry the coffin away it was a giddy blur. We sent Dad off to cremation with a cream donut on his coffin. We had to check we were allowed, but the funeral director said it was fine. Dad loved cream donuts, the proper long ones piped with cream and a coin of bright jam in the middle. We put his pocket knife in one trouser pocket; a handkerchief and a length of string in a neat loop went in the other. Dad always had those three things on him—a throwback to his Outward Bound days—and he made sure we each had them when we went travelling. We wanted to make sure they were with him for the next part.

This seemed normal on that day. I thought about when we studied the ancient Egyptians in school, trapped in a summer room with dust drifting past the whiteboard, and the teacher's drawing of a tomb with all the treasures, and it just seemed utterly normal to send him off with the things he had always carried.

The next afternoon we were gathered in the garden in the sunshine, drinking wine and pretending everything was absolutely fine, and laughing about our cats, which were rolling across the lawn like hairy sea lions. I heard my sister before I saw her, heard her voice say, 'Here's Dad!' and then she appeared, climbing over the hedge holding a wooden box. I didn't understand, and said, 'Where? Where is he?' with my heart in my mouth and my whole body wired like an electrical socket. In less than the second it took her to answer, I had sliced the world apart and looked for him in every molecule around us, entertaining the notion that his death was a terrible dream because she'd just said, 'Here's Dad.' But my sister, her eyes brimming and the choke of a sound in her throat, put the box on the table and looked at me and said, 'Sorry. Sorry, I just mean—here he is.'

I started to cry with absolutely no control, huge heaving tears wet on my legs and on the cracker with cheese in my hand. I looked at the dull blond wood of the box and the name that was his, and his date of birth, and it was undeniably correct. I dragged the box toward me, and it was so heavy it took a moment for my body to make sense of it. I lugged it into my lap so I could turn it this way and that, as if the answer to the weight would reveal itself. It didn't. I sat there in the indecent sunshine, on a wrongly pretty afternoon, and I held that box and I howled. We existed in this day, in the rude health of our human forms, absorbing the sun through our skin and feeling the breeze come through the trees in the garden, and Dad in his box did not. That's how I knew he was never coming back.

After that I couldn't bear to leave Dad's ashes alone in a room. I was worried all the time that he would know and feel sad. I wouldn't allow him to be tucked away like an afterthought, or placed in a room we seldom used. I was always moving him around, as if to show him the house in different lights, the house he built, made for sunshine and fresh air, the house he refused to sell, even as it began to deteriorate alongside him, the decks rotting, the odd window running with water in the winter. I walked with him from room to room, and settled him in sunlight beside the television, or on the kitchen bench or the dining table, on the newspaper still cool from the morning letterbox. I lugged him around, it's fair to say, with the mild desperation of a mule whose job is to carry the load. Someone put him in a drawer when we had our first open home, and when I discovered it I went down to my room, stepped into my wardrobe, drew the door shut behind me, and screamed my lungs out in the darkness.

I took his ashes with me on a car ride to Hamilton, where I was speaking at a festival event. It was the greatest joke I could think to play on him, since on birthdays or any occasion requiring presents he used to inform us that the gift was arriving from Hamilton. 'Any day now,' he'd say, with the sneak of a grin approaching his lips. 'I've had to bring it up from Hamilton.' None of us has spent much time in Hamilton, but we hold a special place for it in our hearts because of this nonsense. Now I put him in the passenger seat and announced, 'Best view for you here, Dad. I'll drive, you look,' and though my voice barely travelled in the closed-in space I kept chatting because I didn't know what else to do.

It was a two-hour drive, just me and my dead dad in a box. I pulled out onto the road, and the car began to make a loud beeping sound. I tried to ignore it; I wondered if it was the air bags, and twiddled with the lights and the stereo. Eventually I had to pull over, worried that the car, a new one to me, was about to explode. I entertained one brief and vivid image of myself blown into chunks, strewn artfully across the bitumen and across the dull grey of Dad's scattered ashes. Perched on the edge of a berm, I searched the internet for 'beeping noise while driving Prius'. It took only a moment to realise that my car thought I had a person in the front seat and this person had been cavalier with their seatbelt. I buckled Dad in and the beeping stopped, and I fell into the first proper laughter since he'd left us. I put his favourite music on, turned it up loud, and we headed south.

———

I understand he is never coming back, but I can't reconcile myself with never seeing him again. I watched him die, I laid my head over his heart and absorbed the silence of him, and I bathed his dead body, but I still don't understand a day without him in it. I can't make my body or my brain understand that he won't just walk in the door one day and give a whistle. It drives me mad. I am a bucket filled to brimming with sadness, heavy with it, pinned to the ground as I am by the loss of him.

The imprint of Dad's body is still in my couch. The shape of him at rest is a shadow on the fabric that remains, though he is gone a year. He lay on my couch, which I'd dragged from storage when we rearranged the house to make it more comfortable for him, for the better part of two years. I'd come home and walk by the living room, and he would always be there, with or without a cat, asleep or awake. He loved that room with the sun streaming in, and he loved my comfortable couch, its soft fabric a kind of oatmeal, its length just right for his long legs, the angle just right to watch the news and to witness the procession of the household going by. From my couch, from right in the heart of the house, he was still participating but without having to get up as much, without having to strain his legs and his lungs.

I walk past my own living room, in a new home farther away, and the couch is there but he is not. My eyes play tricks on me. I think I see him, asleep with his head tilted back, arms laid loose across his hips, hands tucked together, a corpse pose long before he was a corpse, and I flood. I turn to water in front of my stupid couch, which I bought for the first flat I lived in alone. He and Mum came with me to buy it. It cost twelve hundred dollars, and its two pieces came together in a right angle that was pleasing. Dad insisted I pay extra to get the fabric guard sprayed on. Every time I cleaned his vomit off the couch, or a dropped cup of tea or the lurid pink weight-promoting drink he had to have, I thought about that day a decade ago in the shop. In spite of the fabric guard, there is one discoloured patch that I will not try to scrub out. You can only see it in certain lights, and I do not tell anyone. I keep it secret, the halo of his head where the oils from his scalp have seeped into the fabric over time. I lie on the couch the way he used to, and I rest my head in his halo and I think about him. It hurts as if my blood has been replaced by gravel and must pump twice as fast. I turn to grit and I feel my body stiffen with the pain of losing him, and in these moments the grief gets me. It gets me so good I am out for days.

We had thought about death, but we had not thought about the many tiny deaths we would endure in the months after Dad had gone. We attended many small funerals for the life we'd had, and each one wore us down more. We had to sell Dad's boat and it was so awful I thought I would die out there on the marina, just slip into a water grave and be gone. I stood in the hull of our lovely boat and nearly screamed with the unfairness. We kids scrubbed and polished every inch of the boat for the sale. We took out our maps, and Dad's fishing gear; we took out his first-aid kit and his bottle opener shaped like a fish, and his bird-identifying book; and we took our towels and the sheets we'd slept on since childhood, and the ropes from the lockers, and the decks of playing cards thickened with salt and the grease of potato chips, and the nail clippers strung on cord for cutting fishing lines. We erased our presence for the sale. The boat never looked better and we found a grim satisfaction in knowing Dad would be proud. We polished up his true joy, and we did it well.

I felt him close as I stood on the stern. On that worst day, I focused on the green-blue water and watched the swallows skim over it, and a shag glide by, and tried to remember everything we had that was good. When the boat was gone, when the marina berth was sold, it would seal thirty-nine years of life at sea with my dad. On the ocean we never argued. This was the place I came to reconnect with him, a neutral ground of fun and swims and songs on the radio and sunsets. In the mornings, up early to catch the energy of the day, I'd make him tea on the tiny stove, and we'd perch in the stern in our pyjamas, watching the bay wake up, listening to the news on the radio. I knew those mornings were ours, just as the day was, as life was. The limitless wonder of a clean ocean morning and a day holding only possibilities. That boat, which we'd had since I was sixteen, held all the best adult memories I had with Dad.

The new owners were kind, and through some strange twist of fate we felt sure Dad had a hand in, they knew of him through their friends in Australia, the very strangers who'd sold Dad the boat in the first place. They asked for a photo of Dad they would frame and hang in the boat in honour of him. They were so excited to have a boat so cared for and full of good memories. My brother saw them off at the marina and he filmed as they drove it away, out of our pier and into the harbour. I got the message on my phone, and I watched it go and it made me smile for them. Then I put my phone down and cried.

Nobody had told me there would be more cuts and incisions; I'd thought death was the worst. It was May. Dad had been gone for six months and the real pain was only just beginning.

My circadian rhythm is still matched to Dad's and I wake every night at 11.45—awake like a slap—and listen with my blood for his noises across the hall. I listen for the laboured breathing and coughing, and for the moaning in the sleep. I listen for the crashes of falls from bed, and the dry feet sliding across the carpet to the toilet: the endless hallway shuffle and me coming out to help him. I can't shake his night rhythm and I know that a part of me doesn't want to.

We are linked, he and I. Night and day we keep time for each other. It is my job to look out for him. I wake again at 2.30 a.m. and I get up and step across the hallway. In the darkness his bedroom is alive with him. I can discern the smell of his skin behind the candles Mum has lit for the open homes. I can feel the portion of space that his body takes up, as he lies on his back, his old hands entwined, his thumbs rubbing against each other. I can hear him turning in that little hospital bed, and the cough that comes as he settles in a new position when the tumour in his chest protests and squashes his lung. I hear him call out for me, and I turn on the light abruptly and stare at the double bed that has replaced his sickbed. There are too many cushions now, and a coverlet that seems glamorous and untouchable, tucked neatly with pillows placed just so: a frozen room for a frozen home up for sale. I look at the shelves that are empty of his things, of the temporary life he made in the room across the hall from me, his difficult middle child who was in the storm with him those last few months. He is gone. I can't sleep.

We sold the house. It was a dull blow that we were prepared for, and we absorbed the impact like boxers. We curved inwards around the punch to the guts that was signing away the papers to our family home, and we crossed the road to the pub, squinting in the sunlight and shuffling like old people. We drank beer and wine like all the other people in the pub and we said 'Cheers' but we didn't mean it. Now we had to pack up our entire life with Dad and move our memories, and find new places for our feelings that sprang up like weeds in the pavement of the driveway. We made rigorous plans for working bees. We made jokes about the way Dad would have us pack things up. We crawled into bed with dread for company, and our sleep was fitful.

We had always measured the passing of time by dragging out the ladder and shears and climbing to trim the hedges in our garden. Each of us remembers the last time our dad was there to oversee the job, slender in his deck chair but still able to direct us to the places we had missed, and to tell us how smart it looked in the end. We had trimmed the hedges three times since he left, and that was how we knew we were still on the planet, still part of the world that inexplicably appeared to have moved on. The garden was living proof of the passing of time. There it was, brash with life, green and climbing and budding without shame.

The last time we trimmed the hedges before they belonged to another family I leaned out across the top of the foliage and tried to shape it into something resembling order. I tidied and snipped, and the architecture of a design planted many years ago revealed itself again: the history of my family's hope, the garden we grew beside a home that was new to us then. We gathered in the remaining evenings and sat out on the deck with the amber autumn light on our faces, and our smallest humans ran up and down, chasing each other in squeals of freedom. The outdoor table had begun to rot in places, and I lifted splinters of wood with my fingers and remembered Dad's hands. My family were suspended in a golden dream, and in the bright glow of dusk their bodies melted together in a way that made Dad's absence less conspicuous.

We filled boxes like automatons. We packed ruthlessly, yanking tape from dispensers, trying to seal our memories in the boxes so they couldn't escape. We spoke to each other but couldn't listen, played music but couldn't hear it, and ate food we couldn't taste. I watched the hallway as if Dad was coming. I had to be hauled away back into work. I didn't tell anyone I could see his shadow coming up the hall from the garage, the slight tilt of his walk because of his gammy knees, his pause to touch a door frame or address a mark on the wall he hadn't seen. The house was so full of him, and in the activity I felt the tangible whirl of his spirit stirring into life every action he had taken, every day of his life he spent here.

I found a tiny slip of paper on which he had written *Michelle's Room*. It was wedged in the edge of the door frame to my bedroom and must have stayed there for twenty years. I could still see him sanding the doors and getting them ready the week before we moved in, his handwriting so strong and clear—everything about him was always so strong and clear. I pulled out all the Christmas decorations from the cupboard under the stairs, and stood in the dim light and remembered that behind the plaster, right in the skeleton frames of the house, there are five bright silver nails we knocked in for luck, one for each of us, before the builders finished the wiring and sealed the walls. I imagined them twinkling in there, a constellation of us, sending tender light back across the years. One star is dead, but its light remains for now.

I slept with the box of ashes in my arms on our final night in the house, and when I left the next afternoon I didn't look back.

The grief counsellor asks me how I am, and I tell her I'm on percussion in the world orchestra but I don't know what piece of music we're playing. I'm banging some bit of something in the corner and I can't for the life of me tell where it belongs. I am totally out of time. Some days, travelling in my car, I watch everyone going past like they're in a movie. The verisimilitude of my own life passes by me and I note the life going on out there but I can't feel it. The counsellor asks me what the main thing is that brings me here, and I tell her about the last few days of Dad's life. I tell her how I went home one night, just for one sleep in a real bed, and while I was gone Dad woke up and asked for me. I tell her how the ropes around my heart twist tight when I think about it, and how I cannot forgive myself for leaving his side. She asks me to reframe the memory so that my heart can understand that it is not guilt I feel so much as longing—longing to have more time with Dad. She tells me that I am only at the beginning of my grief, and the world yawns open and threatens to swallow me, because it's been eleven months and I am tired. But it's a relief, too; I thought I was being slow. I thought this wet season had gone on too long and I was defunct or I was stuck. I leave the session and brush past someone in the hallway whose face runs with tears. The part of myself made mean by grief is glad to see someone else suffering. In the foyer, children's drawings have been stuck to the windows and they look like stained glass. Many of the drawings have people, and many of the people have wings.

I become unable to answer the telephone. I leave it permanently on silent, without even a vibration. When the home line breaks the stillness with its shrill ring, my heart races. I am primed for calls of urgency. The phone has borne only bad news, and now that he has gone it is news arriving only in apologies, 'sorry' bundled in letters arranged in sentences from people watching us lose.

We are losing. That's what I think when our family gathers for a birthday dinner. We sit festive at a table laden with bright food, but we are losing because we are without him. I know my brain is running rings around me, even as I count the number of us again and again and come out one missing. My brain lays a trap for me everywhere—I am still waiting for him to come back, waiting for the surprise and the joke. I make myself look at the photographs I took of him as he lay dying. I do it so my brain has to remember he's gone. It is like a ritual stabbing. I endure it for a few months and then I stop. I stop looking at photos and I stop talking. I don't answer my phone or take it out much anymore.

My sister and I talk about Dad coming back, and if we could take it, and how it would be. Not back like how he was, is my sister's view. Not that lesser and miserable man. Not that shrunken life running out in front of us. She wants back her old joyful Dad, and she's glad it's over, as terrible as it is without him. The struggle is ended and that's how it should be. Me, I want him back. I want him ill and half asleep and pale. I want to hold his hand and help him to eat toast. I want to help him shave and I want to make him smile. I don't care how terrible it was, I just want to see him again and tell him things. I want to talk to him, and pat him gently, and drive him round and show him the day. I want to make jokes and pull faces that engender only a tiny smile. I want something, anything at all. I met Arun, the love of my life, two months after Dad died. I want them to sit down together and know they are my two best men. I cannot make sense of them never meeting. I don't know how to tell Arun about the huge spirit of my dad. There are not enough words or smiles. I wake in the night and trace the shoulder of my love, and the soft streetlight through the curtain illuminates him enough that I can see his beard, inky dark on grey. I think, Dad will never see your beard. I stare at the ceiling, and think about the whiskers on Dad's face and how life just appears to be cells turning over and hair growing, and the stupidity of it all takes my breath away.

I found the plastic bracelet they cut from his wrist after he died. It is just like the ones they cut off newborn babies in the hospital when they're allowed to go home for the first time. I'd tucked it inside his glasses case, where the frames he doesn't need anymore lie in soft caramel fabric beside a red plastic toothpick with a Christmas tree on top. There is one hair from his wrist trapped in the sticky film of the bracelet. One hair with the root attached: a tiny crescent moon of keratin and a tiny globe of a root, stuck to the inside of the strip of plastic like a bit of biological punctuation. And that's what's left of my dad in real life, what wasn't burned away: one tiny semicolon of hair, waiting for another thought he would never make.

'Everybody dies, Michelle.' That's what a psychologist said to me once, when I was twenty-four and worried, and we sat on leather couches opposite one another in a session that looked at how my brain works. I don't remember the rest of what he said, but I remember that day as a kindly, tired lecture from a stranger about what we endure as human beings, with death the final punctuation to a life littered with difficulties. I suppose it was meant to make me feel that my immediate compendium of hurts was a collective experience and I was not alone. I don't remember taking offence, but I looked at all the framed certificates on the wall, and then at my feet, and thought, Well, this isn't the help I was looking for. Of course everyone dies. That was true then and it's true now, and it's true forever.

I thought about that day often in the months after Dad passed away; I went over the list of things that happen to us all as human beings. There was nothing in that list that explained how to traverse the space left behind by someone you love; how to attach clips and ropes, and scale down into that enormous cavern that is the space my dad left. I tried to read books about death, or about grief. Someone recommended Joan Didion, and I glanced at it and recognised the ideas but they meant nothing.

This grief is not something words can solve. In fact, the English language has failed me, both in the words to describe my love, of which there are never enough, and words to describe my grief. They are the same, because one cannot exist without the other. There is no love without grief, and no grief if love has been absent.

I just go on and on in the wild weather of my own sadness, in this strange microclimate whose nature nobody can predict. One day a terrible storm and the roof lifts from my temporary shelter; another day blazing sun, and my skin bubbles and burns, because I am exposed now, without the shade of my dad, without his umbrella love. I was not really born for a broad world. I was born for the circle of arms that is my family and our adventures together. I was born for sitting on a couch with chips and beer, idly watching TV, arguing and laughing about silly things. I am a family person. And now my family is lesser and our number does not make sense. I had never considered any one of us would die, and I think back to the night my parents sat me down and told me that doctors had found a growth in him, and how I said, 'Oh it'll be nothing,' and I went out for a drink with friends. I just could not conceive that he could be taken down—not really. Knees replaced, a wee stent in a valve, sure, but not anything significant. My dad with his strong legs and sturdy chest, on forever. That was the map of our universe and I knew its lines by heart.

The then and the now are still startling. I am so changed I sometimes hear my voice in a room and wonder who is speaking. The Michelle then, who got the news and went out for a drink, and the Michelle now, who moves through rooms like a wet ghost, with wet footprints, clinging barnacle-tight to love and memories, refining life down to three simple things that matter. Love matters. Family matters. Living things matter. And nothing else. I seek out connections like a sniffer dog at the airport. I am repelled by small talk and time being wasted. I write with furious industry, words falling from me like bricks from a tower, pelting the world with the feelings I can't keep hold of. I write to reach my dad—to reach anyone who will listen. I feel the urgency of my language, and give in to it, waking in the night to write.

Dad's death has changed everything about how I live now. It's like being at a party, in a room swollen with noise and clamour, and someone claps their hands to get everyone's attention and the clap rings through the room, the perfect smacking sound of palms that sends everyone quiet. Dad's death was that to me. Immediate silence. And then, slowly, into the quiet come the new sounds, the only sounds. All the background chatter is gone and into the hush come the things that matter. I am not the same. I do not recognise this person. My face has changed. It's my eyes, which are my dad's eyes—it's what they have seen. They have darkened slightly, as if a storm has settled there. When I smile I feel it in my heart because the smiles are rarer. My body is stiff from sleeps that come in hunched forms, like fallen soldiers. I get out of bed and shuffle for a moment until the blood begins to move around in me, and then I get on with things.

I am not the same, and have no patience and more patience at the same time. There is more patience for the children in my life, who I hold and speak with, and really listen to because it matters. Things that seem trivial make me impatient. I am prone to shouting when something angers me, just shouting to release the tension. I cry over nothing. I begin to grow flowers and plants from seed, cheering on the life that bursts from seed casings and shoots upwards to the sun. Taking it personally when they're thirsty, I water them, celebrating their growth as if they were children. I pull over on the motorway if I see a bag or a box in case it is an animal who has been dumped. In the street I do U-turns when I see a bird in trouble on the curbside. Everything that is alive matters deeply. I nearly smother my cat I'm so invested in keeping her well. She develops a twitch, and I take her to the vet, convinced she will die. She is perfectly well, but she is aging, and the thought terrifies me that one day she will let go of her heavy fur and bones and leave me.

Dad's cat Bailey is older now, and he has dementia and screams and howls and doesn't know where he is. He is losing both his eyesight and his hearing. He was Dad's little mate, and we watch him decline and it is awful, because he is our last link to when Dad was alive and we had a family home and a life together. Now Mum lives alone in her new townhouse, and she has new furniture and new plants and a new life. Bailey isn't in pain, so the vet recommends various drugs to calm him. Hilariously, one is the exact same drug—Gabapentin—that was given to Dad in the latter part of his life to help him relax a bit. After the prescription from the vet runs out, we just break up Dad's pills, which are still there alongside all the other prescriptions he never got through and which we can't bear to throw out. Bailey gets along on Dad's prescription, and somehow that feels right.

In mourning, little things return to you in time. You walk into a room and see a photograph of your dead love, and one day you don't burst into tears. You smile genuinely when you hear some good news, and though it has taken a few months, that smile finally reaches your eyes and crinkles them up at the corners. Even the lines on your face have forgotten how to fold into creases resembling happiness, but they come back. Hope is the last thing to return.

The cruellest thing about the journey with Dad was that we were, in the end, afraid of hope. For a family so optimistic, for a dad so upbeat about the sheer joy of living, it was the most treasured thing you could take from us. Yet, mostly, we would pick ourselves up after each blow and find something to be hopeful about, find a silver lining and gather under it in a huddle of five people desperate for shelter and for sunlight. Yes—this news is bad, it's the worst it can be, but maybe we will get lucky. Surely in the next round of tests they will find something that can help us—a drug trial, some new studies.

I logged in every week to sites that update the world on advancements in medicine. I saw papers about new hope for certain cancers, but we were never the hope story. We were the very rare story, the very advanced story, the if-only-we-had-found-it-sooner story. We had no plan of action because there was nothing to act against, so Dad tried common treatments like radiation 'just in case' and because nobody had any other ideas. 'Just in case' creates false hope because there is always an exception to the rule and perhaps it would be us. Our hope was like a dull cartoon where over and over a character is caught in a trap, blown up by dynamite, tied to a train. We laughed bitterly about the hope we once had, some eighteen months earlier. We resigned ourselves to the worst. We ignored friends who told us to remain hopeful. Ironically, toward the end, when Dad was broken from treatment and miserable beyond belief, we got the impossible news that his unshrinkable, immovable tumour had shrunk. It made no difference that he was some kind of miracle, because he was dying now. My rare dad and his rare disease. It was news too late, and our smiles at this remarkable result were grimaces, and we knew it.

My grief is a shining coin, an Olympic flame, a phoenix rising. My grief is a pet, a limping shadow, a thief. My grief is a sheet hung to dry on a line, and I ripple in earnest with the breeze that blows through me, thin as I am with the missing of him. This bright grief, then—it moves into our homes and we make space for it. We give it its own bedroom, fresh towels, a front-door key. We learn to live with it, and in the echoing vault of loss we take new forms. One by one we evolve because we have no choice.

I watch my brother fill out. I never noticed he was

a half-formed thing, but in Dad's absence he grows taller, and broader, and he fills up the room with his humour. Because Dad is gone, he has permission to step into the role he was understudy for. The protector, the troubleshooter, the comedian. He fills Dad's shoes and the garment of his spirit with a grace that is seamless. I watched him begin to shift at the funeral, where he stood in front of hundreds of friends and spoke of his kinship with my dad, and the time lost, and the lessons learned. He had a drink in his hand and his heart was pouring and he just laid it out there—the trouble and the love. Into the air he wove the history of them, a dad and his son, and all the expectation and disappointment, all the laughter and the regret. In front of us he laid the past to rest and planted the ground for a legacy to grow. And then he did the most remarkable thing. He recited, word for word, a comedy sketch Dad was famous for. Pages of learned emphasis and punctuation, word and inflection perfect. He had us in stitches, and I was open-mouthed in shock because he shifted shape in front of us, doubled back on our lives and swallowed our history, and then he gave it back to us in a new form. My dad living on in the humour of my brother. I had never seen anything like it.

Many months later, my brother still holds the shape of sturdiness and comedy for us all. He is the architect of our way forward as a lesser-numbered troupe. He helps me buy a new car. He shows me how to work it. He gives advice when I'm stuck on the side of the road and confused. He assembles shelves and lifts heavy things for our mum. He makes phone calls in stern tones when he needs to. He goes to counselling and finally addresses his past. He makes us laugh. He cracks our mother up in a way I've only seen our dad able to. He can do this, become this, only because Dad is gone, and though I wish Dad was still here I can't deny my brother's metamorphosis. He is in the sun because the way has been cleared.

My mother wears her sadness as a shield, and she gets through each day with the drawbridge up, flooding from the inside out but sturdy. One evening in our family house when we were alone, she came by my room and hovered in the doorway. We talked about friendships and about loneliness. We were both feeling exposed now, because Dad was the one who brought people together and that was his gift, his connection. She and I are shy people, homely people; how would we get on without our social coordinator? In her uncertain gaze I saw a young woman, swept up in the social whirl of my dad, and his life, and the parties, and the immense fun. That was forty-nine years of her life, and now she must start again. She had never lived alone. Every decision of her adult life was made as part of a two, and now she must assert her preferences alone and find her voice.

As hard as it must be, she does it. In her slow dance with grief she surprises us all. She reaches deep into the wellspring of her own invention and she conjures new friendships. She calls people and asks them out for coffee.

After she moves she makes friends with the widow next door; she joins a society of plant lovers and has board-game evenings. She steps out of the shade onto a bare lawn where she plants, painstakingly, a new garden to keep herself company. I am confused watching her. I don't know how she has done it. I can't account for her bravery, but it makes me grin so hard my jaw aches. She's on her way. She is negotiating the rest of her life without her best friend, though I know she wakes each morning and says hello to him. I imagine her rolling onto her back and looking at the light making its way across the ceiling and recognising that this is another day without her love in it. I see her look at Dad's photo, and turn back the pages of the book they wrote, to settle on a passage of memory. Then I see her get on with her day.

In my mother I recognise the trap that has been set for all of us: the narrative of love that has no happy ending. Our whole lives we are raised to look for love, to yearn for it, to hope for the day we will meet it and know it, and take it for our own. We build our futures on the dream we are sold of an unbreakable two. Find your love, and build your life. There is no script for how to say goodbye. There is no story written about how to stay alive when your love is dead. There is no manual for farewells. I have never seen sadness like I saw in my parents' eyes as they were letting each other go. They gazed at one another and exchanged their lives back and forth in silent memories, and they didn't look away. No words were spoken, but every breath was theirs together.

My sister is the busiest I have ever seen her. She crowds her days with action and helps every single person she can, and in those actions I see how our dad lives on in her. She's so social, and so engaged, and I see this is how she navigates her grief. She does more for people, she tries harder, she loves her daughters even more and goes out of her way to make special moments where she can. She is full of Dad's spirit, and he goes with her through her days, I am sure of it. I see how grief has hurt her, too. 'I don't know where he is,' she says to me, with tears drenching her face. 'Where is he?' She looks for signs, and that's how she negotiates his leaving us. If a song he loved comes on the radio when she is thinking about him, that's where he is. If a swallow appears out of nowhere, that's Dad coming by. I don't know how to comfort her, to show her that where Dad is is with her. I feel closest to him when she is around. I feel him come into the room when she is there with her bright smile and her warmth.

Around Labour Weekend, Dad's cellphone calls my brother-in-law. My brother-in-law is a pilot and he misses the call because he's up in the air. But when he lands, it's there, the missed call logged. There is no way to account for this, the sign we had waited for. Of course, nine months after his death, his number has been given away. We know this, and yet we can't get past the unlikeliness of a stranger, one of millions, calling from that number. What are the odds, we say. I feel sick when I am told the news. I feel so sick I crouch in a bland hotel room in Queenstown, and I have to wait to get up because I feel weak. Dad, I say, into the air-conditioned pallor of a strange room. Dad, where are you? I begin to talk to him, a steady babble of news and thoughts, and I say again and again—I just love you so much, Dad. I wish you were here, I have so much to tell you. For a long time after that I am not the same. I am absent, I am of air. I think about the call each time I'm in a plane between cities, which is often. At the highest altitude I allow myself to consider that phone call, and I decide my dad is up here somewhere, and he thought to try and say hello to our Pilot on one of his trips, when they were in equal territory, above it all. I am not a religious person, but I imagine Dad is up here, up high, looking over us all.

Occasions come. Mum's first birthday without him, when we try to laugh and eat beautiful food that we cannot taste. My sister's birthday, when my card makes her cry because I tell her how proud Dad would be of her. Dad's birthday, when we gather at a nautically themed restaurant and squint in the sunlight, drink beer half-heartedly and find things we can say. Everything just feels hollow, and I know we all remember Dad's birthday last year, in hospice where we had a room to ourselves and I made him the playlist that would become his funeral playlist such short weeks later, and we drank wine and there was cake with candles. I was hungover from a party the night before and the pain of everything made me wince. We took him home the following day, to care for him there, which was his wish. His birthday anniversary arrives and I keep looking at my wrists, which are just like his. I keep wrapping my fingers in a circlet where his wrist band would have been.

In the air hangs the next marker, and the one we all dread and crave: the one-year anniversary of his death. I don't know what I am expecting: misery, certainly, but perhaps some kind of release. Perhaps one year will be not only an end to all the firsts without him, but the start of a new focus and energy. It's stupid to hope for that, but I go on with that hope in the weeks leading up, though the memories come now thick and fast. Into my dreams come the images of the final weeks of Dad's life. So often in my sleep I am in the doorway of his makeshift room again, watching over him, or I'm perched on his walker, just saying good morning and listening to him tell me how he feels. I revisit the day he dies again, and again, and I cannot stop it. I feel the sunlight of that day on my skin, and I remember every single detail with brutal clarity. The memories are hot and tight like a burn on my heart.

Two days before the anniversary of Dad's death, my sister and I go to meet his friends at a lunch. It's a monthly meet-up some twenty years old, founded by our dad, for all his mates who were runners back in the day. As young men they ran marathons all over the world. I remember the smell of sweat and sunblock on Dad's skin when he came home from a weekend run with his friends, out for hours in the midday sun, burnished and strong like a tree. The First Thursday Club initially met to go for a big run around Ponsonby and then down the road to the pub for a lunch. They'd tuck a half-marathon into their working week, and share progress of their families and careers, and trade stories about their competitive running days that grew mythical in proportion. Later, when everyone was too tired or sore to run, as knees and hips gave out, as eyesight and hearing diminished, just lunch was had, and hours of talking. It looked to us kids like real companionship, though we'd roll our eyes when Dad came home and, fit to bursting with memories of when he could run so fast he nearly flew, would tell us he and his mates could still beat us round the block any day of the week. Actually none of us ever did beat him around the block, even as he got a bit older and his knees protested. He thrashed us, and his record remained undefeated.

In the restaurant we search the tables for faces we know. There's a huge table of older gents, but it can't be them, we agree—they look far too old. They look like grandparents, and nothing at all like the bronzed and shining men we have known all our lives. At the bar we recognise one of Dad's best mates lining up to place his order. He shepherds us straight back to this table of older blokes. It is startling to see them all, these men limping to the table, taking a long time to get up or to sit down. There are men with walking frames and canes. One man from a South Auckland running group that has amalgamated with Dad's has a bandage taped across where his nose used to be. It's like seeing the casualties of a war. The war is age, and nobody is winning.

Together down one end of the long banquet table are Dad's best men. These are the young men who knew him at high school, and in their twenties, up to no good at parties. These are the men who came to visit Dad in hospice and held our arms in vice-like grips and with tears in their eyes when they left. They loved our dad and he loved them, and we huddle down the end of the table and sip cold drinks and remember him. In an instant it's like Dad is here with us. His spirit is so alive in their laughter and their memories it is confronting. They carry on with their daft jokes and racket just as if they had never missed a beat, and I love them so much in that moment I can't bear it. That they can tell us so openly how much they miss Dad is the most beautiful and painful thing I have felt in a long time. I keep swallowing the lump down in my throat, and make the best of it, but I want to leave even as I cling to the apparition that they draw in the air with their stories. When it's time to go, through my tears and the glass exit door, I see them ease back down into their seats, wiping their eyes and breathing deeply. It comforts me to leave some grief behind for them to watch over, and to protect.

All this while I have sleepwalked through my days. I am unsure of what is a dream and what is a waking moment, because all the time there is music in another room. It's a quiet piece that goes on, and it reverberates through my body with its tiny strings and percussion. It seems to play at all hours, and I often wake in the night to go to the toilet and hear the strains of that symphony and marvel that it is still going. It is my heart chamber orchestra, always warming up or in full flight. At times it quiets and I can barely discern it. Other days it is too loud and I can't get anything done. Of course I wonder if I have gone mad from grief. Of course I do. I search online for articles about loss. I try to understand time frames, and measure myself against an elusive, imaginary normal.

It is when my family is all together that I see I am in the right place. Around a table we gather in sticky December heat to mark one year without Dad. Every face is flushed with love, but behind the smiles and the jokes and the ruthless teasing that is the mark of my family every face has the imprint of sadness, carrying it like a little torch kept alight. We have been somewhere else, all together, and we have seen something and we are changed. And that's just how it goes, I realise. This is how it goes now. The world is altered and will never be set back to rights. We will go on like this forever, and the semblance of order and the daily mechanism of life will whir and gather us up, and this will be our new normal. On this day, a day I had expected to have some ceremony, I understand that our grief has become ordinary. We wear it like a second skin, like a faded but perfectly fitted tee-shirt we would never throw away, no matter how worn it has become. Dad's ashes and his photograph are on the kitchen table, and we move around him in a domestic dance, stopping to say hello to him or argue about where he should be in relation to the food. He smiles out at us from the photo I love the most because, though taken when he was sick, his gentle smile is full of surprise and true joy. It's a screenshot I took on my phone over Skype when I called him on his seventy-first birthday. Our family had surprised him, and jumped out of the cupboard under the stairs and made a fuss, and he had loved it. Though I was so sad to miss that birthday, the smile on the phone is for me, and for love, and for all of us. It is the smile of my family—joy, real joy, and warm, enveloping love.

I put my head inside the kauri drawer and breathe the sweet dust and leather smell of growing up. Though his things are gone, this old bureau still smells like my dad. It smells like the business cards he collected, bound together with rubber bands, his ink-scrawled notebooks, the clean cotton of handkerchiefs, worn-out wallets, and the dull metal of a pocket knife and some paper clips. It smells like liniment, sweat from sunhats, and salt water that never came out of swimming togs. I rest my chin against the lip of the drawer and I close my eyes and begin to talk to him. I tell him how my cat is, the one he loved so much, and how she tries to get in the drawers when they are open, just as she used to when she was a baby and he was well. I tell him about the sunny day, and the yacht near Mum's new house that's dragged its mooring onto the sand bar. I tell him I'm going to Waiheke for holidays, and how good the swimming will be if we can get any decent days in January. I tell him my foot hurts. I tell him I love him and I wish he would come back, and then I slide the drawer closed and leave the room with his ghost.

Lumen

The fertility specialist smiles and tells me I have the kind of healthy-looking uterus she likes to see, and then tells me I'm probably generating only a couple of good-quality eggs each year. It's not until a few moments later I feel the impact of this blow, feel it make contact with my heart, then bury its weight in my womb. I am still back at the positive news about my nice uterus. Two eggs, maybe three. That's it, that's all, in a year.

The office is set up so that my chair directly faces her, the corner of a desk between us. Arun has to sit on a couch behind me; I can't reach out to him unless I extend my arm back at an awkward angle and dislocate my shoulder. It's like being offered up to a judge who will decide my fate. She reads the information we have supplied back to us in a careful, neutral tone: 'Michelle, you are a forty-year-old woman.' There is a short pause, and I think more is coming, but instead she swivels in her chair to face my partner: 'Arun, you are a thirty-three-year-old journalist and physiotherapist.' It appears that my career has no relevance here; I am a vessel only. I am the sum of my parts: a visually pleasing reproductive system and more low-quality eggs than good ones. While she talks, I feel the room stretch out of shape, and warp to fit every woman who has sat here before me, and who is lining up to come after. It's so perfunctory I have to remind myself of where I am. This is not a meeting with a bank manager; this is a meeting to check about having a baby.

We move on to sperm results; we talk about motility, my age (again), and making the most of chances. When we say we will not be pursuing IVF (we can't afford it, and I am too old to qualify for a free round; we also can't face the miseries we have witnessed in friends), I see her expression change. It is almost imperceptible, the shift that rearranges her features to those of someone who now invests just slightly less. This is the game, of course. This is fertility, where we all run the race; the win is a baby, or you run forever, getting nowhere. Without IVF, we cannot run so far or so fast. Intrauterine implantation—IUI—is our option, and could boost my chance of conception across a few cycles, though its success is more modest. We are not the serious contenders we might be. Still, when the specialist describes the way the sperm gets washed and sorted before being inserted close to a matured egg, I think about lots of cheery souls fresh from a bath, towel-dried and friendly, and I find myself lifted. Should we need it, I could bear it. We move on.

It's not that our fertility doctor is cold, it is not that she is unhelpful or unsympathetic, it's that she is incurious about who we are. Because we are unexceptional: we are two of many, part of the nebulous form from which hopes appear in the shape of babies like misty clouds separating out from the collective consciousness of all who visit these rooms. This is our baby dream coaxed from the air, and it is just one of hundreds and hundreds. We, wistful, wanting, wear our hearts on our sleeves. Surely she notices them beating in front of her. Her eyes range over our blood tests and sperm results; she wields the ultrasound probe with deft precision, and peers at the screen with great concentration, and she examines my partner's testicles with humorous efficiency, but she does not look at our hearts. Perhaps she can't let herself. I tell myself this detachment is a protective mechanism from the weariness of caring too much.

We leave with instructions to have sex as much as we can, because ovulation is imminent. We sit in the capsule of our car not entirely sure what just happened, and go home and hang up the keys and take off our clothes. We start giggling and can't stop. We feel oddly like children—naughty, furtive. I laugh until I cry, and then I sniff for a bit while we have sex. It feels like our doctor is watching us like an omniscient fertility god, nodding at our achievement.

It's all I can think about over the following days, this schedule of reproduction. I am confident we will get pregnant. On paper and on the glowing screen we look good, and we are up for the job. Though we have tried for a few months before this, somehow the new knowledge we have means we'll achieve pregnancy, because we understand exactly what is happening, and when. We will have the sex, we will lie down for no less than fifteen minutes afterwards, we will continue to take our supplements, and we will be pregnant in a few weeks.

I think about that first day and remember how long it took to take off our jerseys and socks, and how we gathered the winter duvet around us for warmth as we lay there, checking the time, checking the pillow jammed under my bottom to tilt my pelvis, talking about work, about our cat, about the future. Now we are deep in another autumn, and the air is heavy with damp, and my body is heavy with the things that don't happen to it month after month. Almost a year has gone by. I don't know where we are.

I find it insane now to think about how terrified of getting pregnant I was when I was younger. The panic when contraception broke, the rush to the pharmacy for a pill to make everything better, the endless years on drugs to prevent life. I was so studious about avoiding the situation I now covet. When I look at the statistics, it seems miraculous that anyone gets pregnant at all. According to the reading material that eyeballs me from the kitchen table, each natural cycle I go through provides me approximately a 5 percent chance of pregnancy. A decade ago I had about a 20 percent chance. Before that, more. My fertility has slipped away quietly, like a boat slips its moorings and drifts, found later where it shouldn't be, worn down and rusted.

I think about the sex ed talks we had at intermediate school when I was eleven, and how they explained our periods to us, and how we left clutching samples of tampons and pads, feeling radiant with our own biology, feeling secretive, and bestowing the boys in our class with mysterious smiles because of this gift we now had, this ability to bleed or grow life every month. The things we were now capable of were dazzling. We felt the power in our bodies, and we paraded our new knowledge around the netball courts at lunchtime, and crunched in groups under the trees, taking apart the little gift packs of sanitary products, admiring their order and practicability. Watch out for unprotected sex, the brochures lectured. Watch out for pregnancy. We read aloud from the pamphlets and tried to imagine having sex. I was fearful of pregnancy, yet was so naïve that a misreading of my sister's *Dolly* magazine meant for years I thought the hair between my legs was 'public'. When I became sexually active I made it my work to always be accountable, to be vigilant. Now here I am, half a world away and desperate to be irresponsible.

The first time I got my period I felt exactly as I feel now: disappointed and sore. Mum excused me from the table, and took me away to the bathroom. I suppose she saw how uncomfortable I was—I'd been complaining of a sore stomach all afternoon. I walked out of our kitchen, left my spaghetti and meatballs wallowing on the plate, and felt the shift in my life. Even though I was joining a club, and finally in the same league as my older sister, who seemed so knowing and so cool, I had the sense that I had lost something. I had responsibilities now. I had tipped over into the next part of my life and there was nothing I could do about it.

Now, too, I bleed and feel disappointed and sore, and I know I am tipping over into the next part of my life—into my middle age. I can't slow it down, and I can't prevent it. One by one my eggs leave my ovaries for a brief dance through my body, and when they are not solicited for further activity they break down, and are shed, little ghosts of the lives they could have been, gone. Someone once told me that you only have a certain number of heartbeats assigned to your body for your life. I don't want to know if that's true, but I think of them running out the way my eggs are running out, and these days it feels as if my heartbeats hold hands with my eggs and they leap off cliffs together and vanish.

It's not a long time in the scheme of things—just a glimmer on the calendar year—but it feels like an age, and my body carries with it the grave fear of statistics, and of the pain I have seen friends endure, and I panic. We wanted to get the jump on any problems we might have, and not wait for a year before looking to see everything was in order. Everything seems fine in the numbers and on the scans, but overnight I have become fixated, and I pore over my test results and think about my body with every waking breath, and I worry.

—

Because I have a series of ultrasounds, I can discern the shape of my uterus as it pulses in and out of shadow on the little monitor. My womb looks like a cave, and the wand of the ultrasound is the flashlight of an explorer, sending light across the walls, looking for the ancient information my body stores on its insides. At one point when they are trying to flush me with dye to check for blockages, I scream in pain and we have to pause while I fight not to faint. The room spins, and I hear someone talking about my cervix as if it's a child doing well in school—just as we would expect it to be—and I lose my composure and cry. I go home and I look up anatomical images of the uterus, and look at the cervix and feel staggered there was equipment anywhere near it. These images are much more detailed than the slick drawings that accompanied our talks at school—every part of the female anatomy is carefully labelled and explained. That's when I learn the cavity in the uterus is called the lumen. I study the ovaries which appear hung at the end of the fallopian tubes like buckets. I'm reminded of the way people carry pails of water from a wooden yoke strung across their shoulders. I visualise myself walking, and see eggs spilling out of my ovaries like water sloshing over the rims of the buckets and scattering everywhere, wasted.

Early on, before the fertility specialist, my GP did something wonderful for me. She told me that trying to have a baby at my age can be an awful time. She said it would be hard, and that I would find myself watching the months go by, and her whole person radiated empathy. It seems funny to call this wonderful, but I was so grateful that someone was honest with me. With the exception of friends who struggled with fertility and laid it raw for me, nobody could just look me in the eye and tell me it was going to be tough. I have lost count of how many people uttered the world's least helpful phrases: 'It will happen when it's the right time' and 'You just need to relax and it will happen.' I cannot calculate my frustration when I hear those words. I want to explode like a dropped vase and litter the room with glass, I am so dangerous with anger about the insipid and lazy use of language. Silly me, of course! I'll just pop over there and relax and it will happen. What a relief to have been reminded of it! It is as lovingly misguided and infuriating as the phrase 'Everything happens for a reason'—to which

I like to look people in the eye and ask the reason why my dad died slowly and miserably of a rare cancer. Reason has nothing to do with it. Everything happens. That's it, that's the end of the statement. A friend told me, when I went on a rampage about it, that people mean well really, to which I replied, 'It's not good enough to mean well. Think about what you say before you say it.'

(I am angry often.)

When my dad died I was angry that someone so good could have it so bad, and have to leave. I was angry that so many indecent humans were thriving, and my best one declined and I couldn't hold on to him. Now I feel angry at the words said by people who have never had anything bad happen to them, and who don't know how to listen with empathy, even though I know we are all trying to find meaning or hold on to some kind of faith in this life. I'm angry that I had to wait so long to find my love, that I may not be able to have his child. I am angry at my body, which I do not understand, even though I try so hard. I am angry at myself for being angry; angry at the trap I find myself in where the anger causes stress, which in turn causes fear that I will not conceive because of the stress.

Every time I get anxious, which is often, I feel the element turned to the hottest temperature inside me, and before I can stop it I see the contents of my womb incinerated in a flash of heat. I lose sight of the rare miracle of love that has arrived in my life, late but perfectly formed. I forget to appreciate the good fortune of finding him, obsessed as I am with what I am willing my body to do.

My GP was encouraging as she laid out a plan for me—for tests for various fertility markers, and for supplements, and for approaching a specialist if I wanted to. She was robust as she repeated these things to me, and prepared me, and felt worried for me at the same time. I am almost forty-one and grateful to have at last found the person I want to have a child with, but it might be too late. Or it might not be, she corrects me, and she boosts me with stories of later-life pregnancies and how much more common they are these days. 'It's a dream to think we all find our partners while we are young,' she says, and then she tells me about how she went to a conference on fertility, and how the lecturer, a man, talked about geriatric fertility, and made a flippant comment about how women shouldn't be so choosy when they're young and should just get pregnant to whomever they could. She tells me this and for a moment we just gape at each other, mouths slack and foreheads creased in disbelief. I let out a squawk like an indignant bird, and she nods and tells me she still can't believe it.

I have never wanted to be a parent on my own. I see it work for others, and it is a marvel, and it is beautiful, but I have always known I'm not capable of it. I only ever wanted to do this in a partnership. So to be judged by a male for perceived fussiness seems like a perversion. As if I have made this ill-advised choice to wait for a family unit and must suffer the consequences of my ancient womb.

I feel the glory of youth around me so often these days. The power of younger women in their fleshy, fecund skins is both wonderful and a torture. In a way I wish I could transplant my brain into my younger self, and impart to her this fate for her aging body, and then perhaps I would have tried harder to keep love when it came, rather than pushing it away. I have no currency here anymore; I feel at this age that I am of little value—too old, perhaps, to bring new life in, but not old enough to bestow any true wisdom upon the world. I am in a limbo, an invisible wasteland where I do not flourish, and where I wait. We don't set a time limit. My doctor tells me to just go on trying every month and hopefully it will happen. I leave her office with a prescription for folic acid, and go home to start trawling the internet.

—

I lie on my back with my hands folded across my stomach and visualise the cavity in my womb. A lumen, like the many others in the human body, but here inside my reproductive system, a space for life to grow. One by one I allow small points of light to appear, glowing softly in that darkness like candles lit at a vigil. *Lumen*, of light, from the Latin, *lumen*, an opening, from the same. I imagine doctors centuries ago, pulling apart bodies and peering into the tubes of the human system; assistants with tapers trying to illuminate secret structures to better understand their shapes and functions. Into the dark openings, bearing light, come the medical practitioners and the beginning of knowledge. Now we can go into the tiniest, most quiet spaces of the body and examine them. We have answers and methods, rescue attempts and exit strategies. The human body is a conquered land, and yet these centuries of knowledge might not help you. You can do everything they tell you to do, and still come out with nothing.

It is not good to know too much. The internet groans with a billion imprints of lives and stories and dead babies and decaying eggs and missed chances and foods to increase fertility and advice on keeping your genitals cool and miracle conceptions and medical misadventures and commiserations about IVF. I can't look away; eventually I find myself able to trace every living moment in my twenty-eight-day cycle, and repeat it perfectly. On any given day I could tell you exactly what my reproductive system is doing. I listen to my body the way you listen for a gas leak—with furious concentration, and fear. I discern the surge of hormones that flow through me around ovulation, and feel them pull away again like a tide, leaving me flat and parched. I imagine I can feel cells dividing and implantation occurring. I detect a slight swelling of my breasts and think it might be an early sign of pregnancy.

Every ache in my abdomen might be a sign of life, every hearty food consumption might be a craving. It gets so bad that when my period arrives I am crushed and confused. The drawer of my bedside table is a graveyard for pregnancy tests. I no longer trust my own body. I wouldn't know a real physical cue if it slapped me across the face.

What makes it worse is the missing out. The whole country cruises into summer. The days lengthen with warmth and cheer, and the collective sigh of five million skins sucking up vitamin D is audible across the land. But I'm unable to relax and not even really allowed to drink. I feel depressed, afraid of the two-odd weeks of waiting after the ovulation period. Uncertainty stretches on, endless, and into that space I project all my fears and all my hopes. I'm not a big drinker, but knowing I can't or shouldn't have a drink makes me rebellious, and it's all I think about. I'm like an octopus prodded in a rock ledge—I come out, limbs flailing, a swirling mass of resentment and flashes of danger. I am dangerous.

In the interests of improving my egg health, we have cleared our home of things that might be harmful. I had never considered how many common household products contain chemicals, or are made of substances that could affect reproduction. In a frenzy, I chuck out almost every skin product I own in favour of ones that won't disrupt my endocrine system. Gone are the expensive beauty products that make my skin look good but contain harmful unpronounceable ingredients. I stop wearing perfume and come to know the true scent of my skin. I feel naked, and in my nostrils is the faint smell of honey, always, from the wraps we now use to cover food in the fridge. Gone is the plastic wrap, along with the plastic containers and the plastic cooking implements. We take the supplements suggested to us, lining up capsules and gels on the bench. I become surly when I try to reduce how much coffee I drink, but in spite of it I begin to take on a shiny sort of glow, and my skin is dewy and my eyes are clear. In short, we are very healthy, and we go for walks up our local maunga in the evening and breathe the air, watching the sun set across the city, and we are connected and close in this endeavour.

Two months later I start picking fights because I am frustrated, and because I am sad about the rush we have to be in. Our relationship is quite new, though it felt like home from the first moment I saw him. It has been giddy and lovely, but it has moved quickly to make the most of my diminishing fertility window, and I feel embarrassed, not because of the age gap of seven years between us, but because I am closing in on the end of my childbearing years while he blooms in relative youth. We wouldn't have to rush like this if it weren't for me. The natural way of things is circumvented because of my body.

One morning in bed he tells me how he danced at a party the night before, and I lose my temper completely. It was a work do, a bit drunken, and largely cheerful because Christmas is coming, and he danced, which he should, and which I would have too had I been there. For some reason this news destroys me. I have never seen him dance, and I never knew him when he was younger, raving away on the weekends, loose-limbed and light in the way you can only be when nobody needs anything from you. Now here we are trying to grow human life, and I have missed out on the dancing and the casual drunkenness and all the levity and sweetness that come from no expectations. I am so miserable I turn it into a fight, and then a feud, and then a stalemate because I don't know what else to do. I hate this rush we are in, but I cannot stop. I hate the biological clock that is the stuff of every cliché, because it is true, and it is a clock made of pins that stick in me with every second that passes. If there is a chance for a baby I want to be here for it, waiting attentively with everything I have, but it doesn't mean I have to like it.

I try to talk about the urgency I feel; try to turn it over and examine it from all its sharp and sudden angles. I am afraid of a life without a child, a life I had barely ever let myself dream of. In public I have always brushed off the idea of children, and never let myself say out loud that a child would complete me. I am always fighting that idea, because of how it diminishes women who are unable to have children, or choose not to for myriad reasons. It seems like a betrayal of the fight for equality to admit that it's this primary reproductive function that I yearn for, that I sense will satisfy me, that I reach for in dreams where I hold a faceless child I know is mine.

I go to auditions for the role of Mother and feel

diminished among these women who have organised childcare to get here, and who check in with each other about how their kids are. I hear the often-repeated words about not knowing real love until you are a parent, and feel the wince of shame and longing. When my dad died, these feelings flooded up like a dam bursting. Here was the family my mum and he had grown, this sturdy unit of love, united these forty-odd years, three children and two parents, and I could see what this belonging truly meant. I felt the handing over of life down generations, and I felt our love pool together in a lush softness that covered us all. It was all we had in those last days, and it was more than anything you could build or buy. His death brought the clarity I needed.

We take a break for a month, even though the month we're not trying might be the month one of my good eggs goes sailing by. I am too worked up inside, I've started too many fights and I need to rest. We have sex just for the enjoyment of it, and it feels like a revelation. I feel my body come back to me and my nerves settle. On holidays we bask in the sunshine and read books and swim, and I drink cold wine in my togs and feel myself come to rights. I think that when we start trying again next month I will carry this sense of calm happiness with me and things will be easier to bear. I write out a plan for when I get stressed, and visualise drawing a blanket of light up over my stomach, shielding the area from difficult feelings and pressure.

I make myself buy a multipack of pregnancy tests, instead of the more optimistic single. I prepare for the long haul, and tell myself I can endure this. I hold visualisations of my womb in which a little life blooms, and breathe and wait, and look at all the different websites for baby clothes and accessories. I know not to get my hopes up, but each month the chance comes, and with it all of the lovely dreams, and I can't stop myself. I can no longer tell if thinking positively is useful, but it's better than just being worried. I find myself buying an oversized denim pinafore and blouses that would work for breastfeeding. I allow myself these things because it is a sweetness I need.

—

Every writing teacher I've ever had has said *For sale: baby shoes, never worn* is the saddest short story in the world. I remember the first time I heard it, in a cool classroom with linoleum floors and a whiskery teacher who wrote it on the board in scrawling handwriting. I was thirty years old, and my friends were just starting to have children. That simple sentence took on a new resonance, because now was the time we were beginning the next part of our lives. Loss like the one in the story seemed unimaginable. Not us, we thought, not us. The class murmured appreciation, and we all wrote it down, and considered its poignancy, its finality. Now I open my wardrobe and see the pinafore with its helpful button access down each side, and wonder if *For sale: maternity clothes, never needed* might be sadder. I hope I never have to find out if that's true.

Times Like These

The ocean does not love me. Though I feel a swell lift the volume of my blood each time I think of the sea, I know it is both fear and wonder working. I was conceived on a boat. Days shy of being born on a launch in the Hauraki Gulf, I nearly killed my mother in the hospital instead. I have salt water in my veins, and it speaks of the depths in the harbours around the land I live on. It speaks as a prophet, as a shell held to my ear. It tells me stories about mortality, and I hear its briny scratch like a blizzard inside a fridge. The ocean loved my father, who spent all his life trying to be closer to it. He'd sit half out the top hatch of our boat, using his feet to steer—one foot to keep the wheel steady and one to push the throttle—while his torso was exposed to the sun and the air. Beaming, he'd take in the vastness of this blue country.

Our boat *Bayseeker* was a tiny Pelin Empress that leaked like a sieve but danced on the waves. It had brown plaid curtains that began to rot in bad weather, and beds tucked away in the hull where we slept side by side, salt-packed pilchards rocked to sleep by the lull and slap of the ocean. On summer evenings we were always up past bedtime, fishing for sprats off the duckboard in the dark with just a torch to see by. My sister held the light close to the surface and we'd watch as teams of fish came crowding. Dough bait made of flour and water stuck to our hands and our tee-shirts, and made nets of our hair. We ran fierce in those summer months. I barely saw a pair of shoes; the heels of my feet were thick, broken-in by clambering on rocks and in and out of dinghies.

On the boat we learned about living and dying. We stayed close to the weather and the waves for a month every summer, listening for wind warnings, sheltering in bays when we needed to, occasionally moving in the night when the weather got up. Mum would hold a big spotlight and angle it ahead in the dark water so Dad could see where to drive. We kids sat hunched and excited in the cabin, feeling the boat lunge through bigger and bigger waves. In the morning we woke to calm moorings, but my parents were silent, my mother tight-mouthed over her cup of coffee. Dad listened to the weather forecast and studied his maps; Mum counted heads to make sure we were aboard. Things could go wrong, we knew. Boats sank in bad weather. People were lost.

—

I fall between two tethered boats neatly, almost like an apology. There is no splash, I just slip silent from view, and the apple I am holding thumps against the side of the boat. In the slim space between the hulls I open my eyes. I feel myself suspended just below the surface, and I watch my gold hair spread out around me, every strand assigned to swim. I watch the apple with its waterlogged teeth marks spin and bob away. The late-afternoon sun fills the water with crystals, and the sound is a wet choir singing. Lights crowd my vision—long, yawning lights in violet and green and white. I watch my fingers reach to touch them and notice my skin is translucent, as if I am dissolving. In the second before they pull me out by my hair, I am everyone and no one at all, waiting to manifest in brine and bubbles. I am five years old and the closeness of death makes me mute.

—

To a point, we aimed for self-sufficiency. Every day we caught fish, or picked shellfish off the rocks, and Dad hauled scallops and crayfish from the bottom when he went diving. We watched him pierce fish through the head, to kill them instantly; watched the sprats we caught swim in buckets until the life wore out of them, and they turned their bellies skyward and died. Then we used them for bait.

Though we were only small and the youngest of us could barely walk, we learned how to impale the sprats through the eye, and back again through its pair if the hook was big enough, so the bait wouldn't loosen too quickly and be lost.

In the evenings we ate the fresh catch, and remembered their lives as we savoured them, fried in a pan with butter, squeezed over with lemon, buttered bread beside them. We wasted nothing. Dad took the guts out and used them for burley bombs, which he'd plunge into the sea in a container full of holes, turning the water to a bloody churn to attract bigger fish in deeper waters. Out there we'd dump the mussel shells, knowing they'd bring curious cruising fish our way. The only time I recall my dad laying a net, we caught a stingray. He cut the net away around its huge diamond form, but couldn't free the tail without risking the barbs. I crouched on the duckboard and watched him hack away at the tail, his mouth set in a grim line. It was miserable, and we let the body go back to the sea, watching it sink slowly until it was gone. Eventually, the brand-new net was put to bed in one of the lockers. I never saw it again.

We loved stingrays. Dad would pull us out of the water if big ones came by while we were snorkelling, encouraging us just to stick our faces under to see the way they moved, their wings sweeping slow as they came in to the rock face and travelled up it, skimming for food. Mum got us a subscription to *National Geographic*, and the month they did an article about stingrays I stuck the photographs all over my school books. In winter I looked at them and remembered the summers with them close by. Later, we would swim above stingrays with confidence, taking care not to put our feet down in sandy coves where they might be cruising for a meal. We'd eat our lunch and watch them swooping silently through the water, and I'd see the knife hacking through the cartilage and feel remorse.

We had dry stores packed into the little cupboard in the galley—crackers, tins of tuna fish that we hid in the back so as not to jinx it, flour, sugar, tea and coffee and Milo, dried spaghetti, tins of peaches and apricots for when the fresh food ran out. Every now and then we'd make land, rowing our dinghy up the inlet towards Coromandel township, all the way up until we could drag the boat onto dry land and walk the short distance into town for the newspaper, any fruit and vegetables we could find, and double-decker ice creams which we ate in the hot sun, careful not to let the melting drips meet the asphalt. On those days we felt like visitors from another land—one that rocked and rolled—and we'd stand in line at the dairy and feel the linoleum floor swell under our feet. We were allowed to buy lollies that could last us another fortnight, and we chose K Bars mostly, their fruit toffee rock-hard, capable of being twisted into shapes, each one lasting two or three days if we rationed it. I could never wait to get back to our boat, even though it was small for the five of us. Out there on the water we made our own rules, and days were governed by tides and daylight, a natural order that didn't feel like an imposition.

On the boat we learned ordinary magic. We made volcanoes out of sand, and Dad lit a fire in a passageway he carved with his hands, sending smoke up into the evening air while we ate sausages on the beach. We dug swimming holes and let the tide fill them, clambering into the sandy pockets, laughing and whooping, Dad submerged holding a can of beer, Mum looking on amused. At Easter my parents found inventive ways to hide our eggs, wrapping them carefully and putting them in dive bags weighed down with sinkers, tying them off the cleats at the back of the boat so they hung in the cool morning water. We had to haul them in, and dry them before we could scoff the chocolate. Our parents used to let us sit in the dinghy when we moved bays; life jackets on, grinning to bursting, we'd cruise behind in our little vessel, the salt air stinging our eyes, the bow waves curling away beside us.

One night Dad fished around in the lockers, brought out a length of rope and fashioned it into a loop. We watched him lean out over the stern, his body tensed, throwing the rope into the dark water. The sea burst into lights, a million stars exploding into the shape of a lasso as he swung the rope back and forth. That was the first time I had ever seen phosphorescence, and in an instant I was aware of two things: the ocean was a vault of secrets, and my dad had the key. He was always like that—no build-up, no inkling of what was coming, just a casual parade of wonder. Here is the Milky Way submerged. Here are a billion lights bothered into glowing by his own hand. We begged him not to stop, and for almost an hour we stayed there gazing. It was impossible to be the same again, and though we crowed in delight with each new shape he procured from the sea—a deep bucket of stars from a buoy, a straight arrow of light from a fishing spear—we were solemn because we would never look at the sea in the same way again. We went to bed glazed with a new understanding.

The second near-drowning has a kind of grace in it. I fall face-first from the duckboard into the night water, into the tentacle arms of my ocean family. The phosphorescent stars show me the way down and I begin to sink. Beside me, the dinghy rope disturbs the water and makes little bursts of light, but my fingers can't reach it. I try to stretch out to grab it, but my limbs turn to seaweed and I slip through the water like a thief. I can hear yelling and the splash of my sister's strong body hitting the surface. Her arms and legs cleave the darkness, commanding it make way for her. The shouting sounds like swimming competitions at the local pool where she dives seal-swift from her starting blocks, where she wins. She grabs me, and for a second we both sink and the bubbles of our breath swarm around us. She grabs the rope and holds it while our dad pulls us in. I sprawl on the duckboard and breathe there. I am yelled at and hugged furiously and yelled at again by my mother, as I breathe and breathe the night air, as salt water comes dribbling from my nostrils, leaving trails across my cheeks. The ocean does not love me but it lets me live.

Of course we learned to swim. In winter we took lessons at Swim-a-rama, the pool in Panmure crowded with weekday lessons. I was in a different age group from my sister, and I held my paddle board and dutifully kicked up and down. I starfished in dead man's pose; I lay on my back and learned to tilt my pelvis skyward so I could float. I was ungainly, and my pigeon toes slowed me down when I crawled freestyle up and down the length of the pool, one foot whacking the other. I was not a good swimmer. I was suspicious of the smell of the pool, the chlorine that stayed in my hair and skin, of water that had no tide and did not change. When we went back to the boat in summer, I still wore a life jacket while I swam. I was old enough to feel embarrassed that nobody trusted me in the water unaided, but I didn't trust myself either. I floated there, supported by the orange bulk of my life jacket, and felt the salt water address my skin. I put on my mask, and spent a lot of time bobbing around, examining the sea floor. I listened to the click of the sea biscuits in the sand, like Morse code, like a message. I couldn't escape the feeling of being coaxed to the bottom. When I experimented without the life jacket, in shallow water, I sank. Around me, the bigger kids in our boat community jumped off the bows, held their breath and dived deep, and I watched them and knew my time was coming. I was passing some kind of test with the sea. We met each day and I floated, and was measured for readiness.

We outgrew our boat and sold her. I climbed up on the wheel of the trailer Dad was using to tow her away to her new home, and laid my cheek against the portside cabin window, looking in on the berth where I'd slept since I was small. I could see myself falling asleep with my cheek against the same window, desperate to be closer to the sea, waking with lines like depth contours on my cheeks. I was worried how we would go in a new boat; at ten, I felt *Bayseeker* was our passport to the ocean, our identifier that allowed us safe passage. How would the ocean know it was us, if we were disguised in another boat?

It is bad luck to rename a boat, but we did it. The name our new boat came with was one we struggled to pronounce. Someone said it was a combination of names made into a new word. We chose *Shakedown*, for a song my parents liked at the time. I know now that the bad luck comes from an idea in sea legend that the name of your boat is entered into a ledger, and the god of the sea knows your name from then on. Changing a name indicates you are trying to sneak something past the sea god and cannot be trusted, and ruin will befall you.

For *Shakedown*'s maiden voyage, Dad went out with my little brother, and our neighbour and his son. He was to come back in the afternoon, drop off the neighbours, and pick up my mum and sister and me so we could go out for the weekend. We waited at the berth in the marina we rented now that we had a boat too unwieldy for a trailer. We waited, and the afternoon sun shifted across the water, throwing us into shade. We waited, and other boats came in and out. Mum paced. We heard Dad yelling before we saw him. He was in our little white and yellow dinghy with my brother and the neighbours, all of them in life jackets, all of them stunned. He puttered into our berth and cut the outboard engine. A submerged yacht that had sunk in the harbour had drifted into the channel; a piece of wire from the mast had wrapped itself around the belly of our boat and ripped it away. Dad had called Mayday for the coastguard, and piled everyone into the dinghy as the boat slowly sank in the channel.

After that it was never the same for my mother on the boat. She was afraid we would die. The boat was repaired, returning to the marina reupholstered and shiny. It had a top deck which we accessed with a ladder, and Mum would use the intercom system to check we had got up there okay, even though we were nimble as monkeys and perfectly safe. The only time she relaxed was when we were tucked up in a bay in the evenings, and even then she'd worry we'd have to move in the night. Dad tried his best to calm her, but he felt he had let her down. He was always checking to see she was enjoying herself, always trying to make it the best for her. In bad weather Mum would sit at the table in the cabin and grip its edges with knuckles so white they went transparent. The boat brought her close to her own mortality, and she couldn't shake her sense of unease.

There is a culture at sea I grew wary of, by way of my mother. Through her filter, I could see the way the boaties drank was excessive, and how she began to dread the evening gatherings in bays, when all the boats anchored near one another, and dinghies ferried the adults from boat to boat as they grew more raucous, more bleary, more rude. Drinking and the ocean go together, a mythology woven through centuries of salt and piratical behaviour. Some of my dad's friends had huge, expensive boats, and every night it was a pissing contest, a display of magnanimous benevolence, as we were invited aboard vessels that had room for many more of us than our own boat. We kids clambered around inspecting the hatches and crawl spaces, the height of the top deck for jumping off, the dinghies. The parents poured drinks, put out cheese and crackers and pickled onions.

Through the windows I watched my mother watching us, her smile wan. She would rather sit out the back and watch us play than listen to the posturing and puffery of these nights. She stayed up after we were in bed, and I know she tallied the drinking, the way all children of alcoholics do, her skin an antenna for trouble. When the men got more boozy and their talk more sexist, Mum, like a sensible siren, drew Dad away to the berths where we slept, to the promises of another morning of fishing and swimming. Our dad was the comic relief, and I fell asleep to the laughter that punctuated his impersonations as he called his goodnights across the water.

I hold my breath as I hold my body rigid, and arrow to the bottom, where the anchors of the boats bite into the sand and the water is cooler. I swim as a snapper, as a kahawai, as a shiny new sprat. I dive starboard to port below the bellies of the boats, past propellers and rudders. I let the hulls scratch my back as I skim below them, and imagine I am a whale ridding itself of barnacles.

Our friends have a new boat, a bigger boat, and its freshly painted hull glows in the water like a beacon. Of course I want to traverse it, even though I can see it is too wide for me, too deep. I gulp air, and propel myself below, only to turn back again and again. The hull is so immense it's hard to see the other side. I find the solution watching a shag sit proud on the end of our dinghy, surveying his wet metropolis for a moment before he dives beneath the waves. On slippery feet I balance on the wooden seat of the little craft and I wobble and consider if it's worth it.

The push from the dive gets me close to the rudder. A few lopsided kicks and arm-drags and I'm crossing the middle. I can see the top of the water and I kick on, spotlit from the bright white of the hull. It feels endless, the kicking. The surface is no closer, and I look at my limbs to make sure my body is moving. I move but do not progress. I twist from side to side to test my body along the water lines and discover I'm snagged. Bubbles of air blaze from my mouth and leave me behind. In growing panic I become an anemone; my limbs flare and contract because I am stranded here, tied to the rudder by the strap of my swimming togs. I am sea-life collected to study: helpless, squirming. I hear the choir come again in rainbows of light. I feel my ribs almost crack from compression as the last of the air leaves me and, desperate, body thrashing, I rip myself away, feeling the fabric of my togs tear at the seams. I leave a strip from the shoulder there, a faded purple flag with silver stars, rippling in the water country where I am an uncomfortable citizen.

At some point, Mum left us. She made it clear her time on the boat was over, her duty done, her children raised almost to adulthood without major injury. It was the first time I'd seen my mother unpersuadable. Though Dad pleaded and cajoled her, though he made veiled attacks on her decision, she did not budge. Her concession to participation was to make sure we had the right food stocked, and that the towels and linen were washed before we slept too feral.

We went out without her, and we took up her roles on the boat with ease, my sister in charge of the cooking, and me in charge of the dropping and raising of the anchor. We played more music now, dancing in the stern some days, and Dad stayed out later on other boats while we swam in the night water before curling up with books and helping him back on board when he arrived, merry, exclaiming my mother should be with us. He missed her, and now he had a cellphone he called to report our activities, as if checking in with an authority. He wanted her to know the boat was safe, and we were well, and we passed around the phone and reported back on our adventures. When we came home she was happy but terse. She sniffed us and told us we stank.

We felt bad about leaving her, but the gulf called to us. We didn't stay out so long anymore, perhaps a week at a time, but we packed it with all the things we loved to do. We were crusted in salt, washed through with beer, and sunburnt. We swam constantly, barely waiting for the anchor to drop before we plunged in. Dad took a scrubbing brush down to clean under the boat, popping up on either side of the hull to remark on how good it would be to have Mum with us, how surely she would love this sunny day, this new cove we had found, the flounder we had caught for our breakfast.

Our land and sea lives travelled on parallel tracks,

seeming never to meet. I divided myself into nautical maps and road maps for the neighbourhoods I explored as I pushed out of my youth, and into university, and then drama school. The ocean was always the answer, but I couldn't spend as much time asking it questions as I would have liked. Dad texted me often, asking if I could make it out on the boat on a sunny day, on an unplanned weekend. I always had work for school, and lines to learn, but I tried to make it. I had grown out of my home, but on our boat, this last boat we would ever own, named *China Beach,* I found my place of happiness with Dad.

We were a difficult combination, us two. We loved each other but we disagreed, and I flared up under Dad's dominant, enormous nature. He was bossy, and so am I. He worried about my choice of career, wanted me to give it up, wanted security for me, and it was an argument we recycled again and again, becoming heated in lean years when I didn't work much, when he helped me out financially. I was always trying to show him the value of art, and sometimes he came to see me act in a play, and his pleasure and admiration was an explosion of joy. Other times he tuned out, didn't want to know. I was his difficult middle child, the one he did not understand, despite his naming me after the Beatles song, despite teaching me how to dance, despite handing down his mad accents and characters and sense of play. I once overheard him tell my mother that I wasn't like the other kids. 'She thinks things over very deeply,' he said. 'She feels big things,

Valerie.' From the hallway where I had paused, I heard the frustration and love in his voice.

I was scared of his temper and his sunniness, which existed sometimes in the same breath. I have inherited his moods and he didn't like to see them in me. But on the boat we were connected. It was not uncommon for him and me to be out on our own. We got into a rhythm together, and it was harmonious, and easy. I got the food ready, made sure we had bread and milk, and the fixings for sandwiches, and Dad was in charge of the gear for the boat, the beach towels and the beer.

Now that he is gone I dream of those summer afternoons, tucked into little bays, our boat swaying on the anchor, and Fats Domino on the stereo. We sing and dance, Dad and I, our mouths full of food, which we grin through and can't wait to finish, because the chorus of the song must be sung together. After dinner we sit with a glass of wine and watch the sun slip away, and the lights on the boats switch on one by one. We don't talk much. Now and then we will hear a fish jump, or watch a dinghy go by, and Dad will ask if I remember something we did on the water back when I was a kid. I always remember. The water is a vault of our memories and we share this key. I make up the beds, lowering the tables, laying out the squabs and covering them with blankets, then sheets and duvets. I go to sleep listening to my dad breathing and the water coaxing music from the hull, and I feel euphoric. This is where we know each other. Nothing can touch us here.

Dad managed to coax Mum onto the boat just for a night, and nobody could believe it. I think she went because it had been years of Dad missing her and she knew how much he longed for it, and because my sister had a capable boyfriend who'd be there too and she felt reassured. I could not go on this trip, and perhaps that gave her more comfort still—the klutz was not in attendance.

I don't know how it happened, but there was an accident. I don't know what kind of bad luck let that happen to Dad on this trip with everything riding on it. Dad got too close to a reef which was marked on the map but not by a beacon in the water. The hull of *China Beach* scraped across it, startling everyone, tearing at the paint, nearly marooning the boat on the rocks. Dad managed to get it away before it lodged, before more damage was done. They did not have to call Mayday and no rescue was required, but it was enough. It was enough that my mother went into a kind of shock and the trip was ruined. That was it, Dad knew. That was the dream of Mum on the boat gone forever. That was the slamming door and the silence.

I went to see them when they got home and it was as if my mother had left her body and gone drifting away somewhere. She did not communicate, but carefully washed and dried the beach towels, and put away the leftover food. I'd never seen Dad so crestfallen. He was like a helium balloon three weeks after a birthday party. 'It's such bad luck,' he muttered. 'It's such bad luck, Mouse.'

There is no boat to go on now, and nobody to ask for a day trip out in the harbour. I have avoided the sea for a whole year in Dad's absence. I went away to Vietnam, to a farther ocean, and could wade into the water only once. It was too connected to him, and to our history. For holidays now I go to Waiheke with my husband, and we stay in a cottage above Palm Beach. I don't tell him that I chose this bay because we never took the boat in there with Dad. It was too exposed and we favoured little anchorages like Garden Cove instead. There is less chance of pain, I think, at Palm Beach.

From the balcony the sea glitters, and I watch the boats come in and anchor and send out their dinghies to the shore. At night I watch the masthead lights come on and I fight off tears. We learned the shape and way of Waiheke from the sea side, not the land. Now I drive the car to Oneroa for supplies and it feels like a cheat. At the dairy I stand in my shoes, and my clean clothes, and I feel nothing—no motion, no difference. I am of land now and I feel wrong in my body. I look for *China Beach* every time we come down for a swim. I wade waist-deep and watch the bay, just in case the new owners might bring the boat in. I duck under and the water is freezing, and I hurry out, and watch Arun throw himself through the waves with a real happiness I recognise but can't access.

On the ferry home I remember the last time we went to Waiheke with Dad, on this same boat, heading over to have lunch in the sunshine. Dad had about eight months of his life left, though we did not know it, and he sat with his cheek against the starboard window, watching the water, pressing his body closer to the sea. He was too thin and cold to stand out the back and let the salt air pummel him. He watched other boats with a keen eye, and pointed out a shag swimming past.

Now I press my cheek to the starboard window and look for Dad in the waves. I think, I will not go back to Waiheke again until I can go in a real boat. My sister and her husband have bought a little runabout, big enough to fit five people, and she has promised to take me out when the weather is good. She sends me photos of my nieces wearing life jackets and holding up the fish they've caught, giving a thumbs-up for the camera. They are replicas of photos of the two of us doing the same things on *Bayseeker* thirty-five years ago. Our grins and shining eyes match.

Form

I walk down the street in early summer and I feel my thighs rub together beneath my shorts. The meeting of flesh feels like a provocation. The shorts ride higher than they used to, just managing to cover the curve of my rounder bottom, their cuffs resting in the shadows below. Above the waist band is a gentle lip, like the rim of a saucer, and it's my fat sitting there, dainty and sweet. In the mirror my face is like the moon, my cheeks filled out, with only the faint edge of a cheekbone discernible under the skin. It reminds me of when I came home from Paris when I was twenty-two, after six weeks of eating pastries and crêpes and the marshmallow chocolate bars you bought from the refrigerator section of the supermarket: I was rounder then, too. I pour my breasts into old bras and feel the straps dig into the flesh of my back. For the first time I have proper cleavage and I can't stop looking at it, marvelling over the difference it makes in my tee-shirts. I feel my torso thicken, feel the space I take up in the world become more permanent, feel the weight of my body where it lands. I lie in bed at night and run my hands over my hips, feeling the softness where the bones used to protrude a little. I am the curved hull of a ship, at sea in my sheets. Everything in me is in circles; I am round in the places I need to be, and plump with the juice of living.

I don't know if I would be in the place I am now had it not been for seeing what a body slowly dying is. In Dad's passing I found something I had lost—a sense of perspective that had abandoned me by virtue of being a woman in the world we inhabit now. When Dad got sick and his body began to waste and he grew thinner and thinner, it changed how I felt about the weight on my bones.

His weight was what first alerted us to trouble, the sudden loss of it how my mother knew something serious was brewing in his body. It is often one of the first markers for cancer. Initially he looked really good; his stomach lost its beery fullness, his face lost some of the jowls. But that was before we knew it was a disease. Then it became a problem, as the diagnostic tests came thick and fast, and the weight kept shedding, while the grapefruit-sized tumour behind his lung bloomed, its cells taking over, taking his flesh away from him as it fed. The round of radiation he had was a shot in the dark, but it still mattered to get it right, so a nutritionist advised us on how to keep weight on Dad. If he got too light, radiation that was meant for the tumour might be directed instead to his precious healthy cells.

I'd never seen someone try to gain weight and fail. Dad couldn't taste anything, had lost his love of food somehow, and it bothered him all the time. He would gesture at his throat and tell us that nothing tasted the way it used to. There were days when we couldn't even tempt him with a cream donut, though he'd try to eat it for us as we hovered. Nothing was tasty, he would complain, though we packed food with salt and butter and herbs. We tried everything we could, buying soft white bread from the bakery, making the best sandwiches of our lives with ham, tomato, cheese, and cucumber sliced finely and doused in malt vinegar. He'd push them away after a few bites. I'd never really seen Dad afraid, but he was now, and I knew in the back of his mind he was picturing his dear friend who had become skeletal before he died of cancer. Dad tried hard not to be like that, because somewhere in his body wisdom he knew that his flesh and his fat would keep him alive for longer. He had to drink bottles of a pink milkshake to give him extra calories, and he hated them and we all hated the smell. Our life in food, previously a luscious, endless banquet, seemed to collapse, and with it my interest in eating. I lived on adrenaline and coffee, and stolen cigarettes, secreted and inhaled in the garden, where I'd remember to breathe, and breathe smoke, and feel not a bit of hunger.

He'd always had these beautiful strong legs, runner's legs, with meaty thighs delineated by ropes of muscles. Knee surgeries hadn't spoilt their beauty, though he hobbled more. The disease stripped them, taking their bulk and their weight-bearing strength. I could see the joints of his knees bobbly with bone, his ankles delicate. I watched his body shrink and be consumed, and felt helpless. Some mornings we would wake up and his face seemed filled out from the sleep and the fluid, but it was only temporary, and would fade. And we got thinner with him. I look at the photographs from around the time of his death, and it's all shrunken people in the frames alongside him. It gave me no satisfaction to fit the smallest clothes, to never have to squeeze my flesh behind a zip or hold my breath to do up my jeans. Our bodies, our hearts, were joyless.

We washed Dad's body after he was gone. The nurse gave me warm flannels and I waited until they were gently warm, not steaming, and wiped my dad's long legs and his feet. I could still smell the scent of Mum's hand cream that I had massaged into them only a day before. I wiped down his arms, and his old hands, and behind his ears, which seemed enormous now, too big for his little body left behind. I looked at the shape of him there in the early-afternoon light, and he was reduced with such finality that it shocked me. I wanted to make him bigger, make him fit the clothes we had for him, and not have his jeans sagging at the bones of his hips, his shirts voluminous, his underwear loose. I wanted to fill him out, turn him back into the shape of a living man. His body in profile was like Tony Fomison's painting of the Dead Christ. He was so hollow, and so still.

When we came through the other side, and our circadian rhythms came back to themselves after many months of midnight wakings and terrified sleepless nights, I began to eat again and really taste it. I ate for myself and for my dad, drizzling big bowls of lentils with oil and lemon, poaching eggs and puncturing them on thick slices of toast, letting the yolks ooze and get on my chin. I filled out as I came a little more alive, and I sought out the food Dad loved, as if to enjoy it for him—peanut slabs, a good beer, some potato chips, an omelette beautifully browned the way he liked it, the soft green freshness of parsley peeping from the inside. I ate and ate, and I felt like I was living as I saw it effect changes to my flesh, as I filled out the way Dad never could, as my bones retreated into the sanctuary of my body and I drew my fleshy veil across myself.

—

I can't reconcile my new form with the expectations I see around me every day. I start to delete the fashion houses I follow on Instagram, because their models alarm me, and I don't know how to not see corpses strolling down the runways. It seems perverse to me now, the ideal we chase of an emaciation that appears close to death. The angularity of limbs, unless they come from gangly teenagers, seem an emblem of decay to me. The less flesh on the bones, the more quickly you will succumb to death, I warn myself, hearing my dad. I have no proof, but I feel my fat is a buffer between my soul and the afterlife.

I'm still not pregnant, yet algorithms send me adverts for diets, assuring me I can lose my baby weight in mere weeks. I look at the sites before I can help myself, and then turn off my phone, disgusted at the easy target I am. It strikes me as obscene that even as we fatten up our babies and celebrate feeding them, the subconscious messages are of our own starvation.

At work someone makes an admiring remark about an actress who has recently had a baby and looks as if she was never pregnant, and I feel my jaw tense with the things I want to say. As if that is estimable. As if your body holding no trace of the life you fostered inside it is a goal. I don't know why we want to erase our experiences of nurture and struggle, and make it seem as if there was never a life inside that human greenhouse, growing gentle in there, protected and nourished. Women are encouraged to erase every trace of the stretch of their skins, the sag of their muscles that parted to make room for new life. It wears me out, this erasure.

We used to run through the Domain so fast we were flying. We were twenty-two, and as we ran we told each other our acting dreams and everything else we hoped for. We ran every single day, then came home and flaked out, watching *America's Next Top Model* on TV and eating chilli mussels from plastic containers, and rice crackers with avocado. My friend's nana used to regard us as we hauled on our running shoes, smiling and telling us our legs were like big strong tree trunks, and we would laugh but flinch inside, because we didn't want trunks for legs, we wanted dwindling limbs, languid in length, and slim. We wanted legs like the girls in *Top Model*, endless and thin. We made up for it by running twice a day, running off the rice crackers and other healthy foods we chose with care.

All around us our friends tried diets: one week only green foods, to alkalise; one week only meat and cheese, to put the body into ketosis. In all the flats where we'd go to party, there'd be diet books and fitness magazines stashed beside the couch or, worse, in the toilet. I don't know if it was symptomatic of the industry most of us were in, but we were certainly in the business of appearance, and it occupied a lot of our time. I felt the duality. The preoccupation with the external felt uncomfortable because I had only ever put store in the things inside me—my thoughts and feelings and values. It was counter-intuitive to me to put so much store in my looks, but I did it, because I had chosen a visual medium, and at some point I'd be showing up for cameras, and everyone feared the lens that made your body more generous. We used to joke that the benchmark for thinness was when people started to ask you if you were okay, if you were unwell.

It's hard to know where you absorb these bodily expectations from. It goes so far down our timelines, it is lost back in centuries when waists were yanked in with whale bones, mammal to mammal, human bones squeezed into the spaces inhabited by organs. It is lost back when strips of cloth were tied tightly around children's feet, binding them so they couldn't grow too big. People say it's the 'patriarchy', waving that word around as if it is the answer to everything that has gone wrong, but I am helpless with that word, and with the history that has diminished us both literally and figuratively. Most of the negative things I've heard about the female form have come from other women. I castigate myself for the time I spend worrying. I can't imagine a life of casual disregard, of not looking and measuring, but I long for it.

I think about the way women are pitted against each other, and compared in a way I do not see happening to men. Maybe we've been down so long we have turned on each other. Perhaps all of this we do is not for men, but for the approval of other women and to win in the silent competitions we engage with every day. I think about the women's magazines that churn through the world every week with their ideals of beauty blaring from every page, and I feel let down for us, and bitter, because I am a participant in the vivisection of beauty, and I don't know how to get out of it. I am a vain feminist and I feel guilty. I want to challenge my brain and get tough on the lack of equity I see everywhere, but I still want to look cute. Every part of our bodies is policed in some way or another, and we are too thin, or too fat, we have tried too hard, or not enough, we have changed too many things, we should just tweak it here or there, we're looking tired, or suspiciously rested, we can eat what we want, we can't eat anything at all. It's so loud in the world of women.

After my growing year, most of my clothes strain at my skin, and at times I feel like my body is a horse pushing at a gate. I go up two sizes in jeans. Dresses that cinched around my waist won't zip up. Mostly I feel good, healthy, happy. My body runs like a nicely maintained machine, and I sleep, and my eyes are bright and my heart rate is steady. But I know I have to go back to work on a job for which they took my measurements six weeks after Dad died, and I start to watch the conversations that pop up in my head. I notice when the language I use turns towards the negative, the accusatory voice that critiques every part of me. One day I make a rueful comment about my weight to a friend, and she looks at me with a firm expression, and says that in her house they don't make negative comments about their bodies. I am embarrassed and grateful for the way she has made it simple, and for the way she is protecting her daughter from the conversations women can so easily fall into.

I make a conscious effort to change it. I temper my language, making note of the words that condemn me, and try to shift them. Then I try to erase them as talking points, pushing the body object further down the line of discussion until it barely registers. I don't always win, but it feels better. In those times I remind myself of Dad, and how hard he tried to stay on the planet, feeding his body to avoid the firmament with every effort he could spare, and I feel the snugness of my clothes against my flesh and make new vows. When the wardrobe department contacts me to ask if my measurements are the same as last year, I am quick to say no. I have no scales and never weigh myself, so I can't give them an accurate idea, except for the size of my jeans now. In the end I make it simple. 'I'm just juicier,' I tell them. 'I'm juicy, you'll see.'

Every audition we receive as actors begins with some kind of physical description, and possibly a request to wear tight clothing to show off our figures. I can count on one hand the auditions I've done where the brief addresses only the spirit and history of the character. Until you are old enough to stop being a figure who invites lust, you can't get away from the pressure to conform to a tidy figure, to maintain your weight through the off seasons. Because we are contractors, there are many off seasons, and we're expected to be match-fit all year round, it's just how it is. I often think about the roles I have played—so many sirens, so many sex-mad vixens—and feel I have been set up to fail. If you're always playing the bombshell there is an expectation of how your body will be, how your face will remain unaged, and all the while everyone watching like a hawk for when you slip up.

—

At an awards night, a man smiles and asks me when I am going to let myself age, and I feel the slap of reproval even as I receive the compliment. The expectation of how I will age is a tightrope I walk, is the close mirror I peer at, is the shop windows I walk past, looking, looking. I feel the duality in myself with every breath. I want to get older, but I don't want to give in to aging. Even the words 'give in' have an attitude, as if the surrender to time passing is a defeat. I would not go back to my younger self for anything, but it seems cruel that the exact moment I learn to feel good about myself, when I wake up and my thoughts are directed kindly towards my being, that's the exact moment youth escapes me. I watch it go, my youth with unlined skin and lean legs that do not ripple with cellulite. I watch it leap through meadows, and I do not want to run alongside it, but I envy it. The irony is not lost on me that in your moments of greatest physical radiance you can feel your most diminished and insecure because you don't yet have a sense of yourself, and in the moments of your best wisdom gathered around you, when you have stopped fighting yourself, that's when the lines come, when your body is less elastic, and you don't want to go outside lest someone sees how tired you look.

——

It's a very attractive trap I have got myself into, and I feel helpless as I watch my body and face begin to age. I can't keep up with those expectations anymore, and I don't even want to. It was always a surprise to me, who got around in track pants and glasses, free of make-up, in old sneakers, that anyone would see me as a siren in the first place. I have always been a bit of a tomboy, living in jeans and jerseys. I am desperate to play characters like me, with rowdy inner lives and questionable fashion choices. I feel myself teetering on the knife-edge of middle age, and the green pastures of invisibility call to me: there I can stroll undetected, and my work can be offered on the merit of skill and not looks. But I am still auditioning for bombshells, for women younger than me. My age range on my agency website reads 34–44, and when I try to have it changed I am assured I could still look thirty-four if I wanted to. I do not want to. I am ancient on my insides from all the things that have happened to me, and I see the age and experiences in my face very clearly. I see the age in my body, where it thickens and becomes stubborn, where my muscles soften and my skin changes its texture. I feel stuck in a limbo where I'm too old to play the object of desire, but not old enough to play the characters I want to play, who have let life happen to them. I sit in this limbo and dream about the time when everyone will forget about me. I pour my living energy into writing and I foster my brain, which only grows bolder and does not diminish with the years.

Some days it feels as if the collective fear of aging wants to paint me all over with correcting fluid. We are so homogenised now in the way we want to age that we can't recognise a naturally aging face when we see one. The faces growing lined and older are the ones we are suspicious of, the ones that stick out and alarm us—we are so used to the smooth, plumped faces of women in their fifties who look twenty years younger. The standard of beauty will always be youth, but alongside that now is a cookie-cutter face you would know anywhere, because you see it on everyone who has visited a cosmetic clinic. Those Real Doll lips plumped and primed for activity, the smooth tight foreheads and winged brows, the cheeks full and round. Everything injected to replace the fat that has been lost in the body—that youthful fat whose presence is itself anti-aging.

Many women I know have softer skin than babies'. Some women I know look like babies with very old eyes peering out, and it gives me nightmares because I am complicit in what they do. I spend so much money on skincare that my accountant sends me a note after a tax return and asks me if the amount of money I'm claiming is correct. It is correct—I'm a skincare junkie, and think nothing of the bills I rack up trying to nourish my skin and reverse the signs of aging. I am a walking contradiction, because the actresses I love have lines on their faces, carry weight, are human and vivid and complicated, but somehow I can't quite give myself permission to be that too. Not yet, I think, but soon. Except the soon is here now, and I know it matters what I do with it. It matters for my spirit that I accept with grace the way things are beginning to go. It matters for how I want to represent myself as a woman, and the things I will no longer put up with.

The one thing I will not change is my pigmentation. People have been trying to get rid of my sun damage for decades. Every time I go to get a facial, beauticians assume I have come to do something about the freckles that drift across my forehead like clouds, that splodge the sides of my face like new rain hitting asphalt. We are an olive-skinned family who turn the colour of jacket potatoes in summer. We are freckled, all of us; freckles like crowds gathering near our mouths to witness our grins. My sister and I have birthmarks on our thighs, and I have one in the edge of my hair. They are the exact colour of the skin of an almond, and they mark us as who we are.

When I tell beauticians that I'm not here to correct the pigmentation, they look confused. When I venture to tell them that I like my freckles and I don't want to do anything about them, a look of distaste forms in their features the way skin forms on a cooling mug of Milo. Quite recently a make-up artist on a show I was working on said she had never seen me without foundation before and she hoped she wouldn't have to again. She laughed, and warned we must never hang out unless my freckles were covered. She said it jokingly, but I knew she meant it, because when I told her I liked them and I didn't want her to try and cover them up, she said 'Oh!' with a look of absolute shock. Nobody can understand why I want to keep them, these constellations in brown. What I don't say is the lesson I receive every day from my melanin.

The freckles showed up in a seminal year in my life when, at twenty-six, I lived in South Australia, and worked for many months out in the countryside under the hot sun. Most of the cast were women, and I absorbed so many tricks about how to be a woman from them. They gave me advice on skincare as I wrestled with pimples and an oily complexion, and they gave me advice about which birth-control pills to take if I didn't want to put on weight. I followed that advice, which seemed so obvious and helpful, and I took a different pill, and that's when my freckles came. They call it melasma, the pigmentation that comes out because of hormones. It came thick and fast, and it moved across my face in clumps of brown so evident that my nephew asked me why I had rubbed dirt on my face. The doctor hadn't told me that while this contraceptive was good for weight control, the appearance of melasma was a side effect. The clouds of pigment migrated across my face, moving all the time. Once, they settled above my lip like a moustache. I was horrified and sought help, but aside from lasering my face there wasn't much I could do except stop taking the pill, which I did. One skincare specialist said it would probably all come right after I had a baby and my hormones settled. I tried the laser, which stung so much I sobbed and sobbed. The melasma turned almost black and flaked off, and for two weeks my skin was like porcelain, but then the pigmentation came back with a vengeance.

Fifteen years later, the clouds have settled high on my forehead, and they darken for about a week each month when my period is due. That's when I notice them most and remember that time when I was young. And that's why I don't want to erase them. They remind me of the things I tried to do to my body, to control my weight, to monitor my appearance. They are my living lesson, and I appreciate them. There is a large sunspot on my left cheek, high on the curve where it meets my eyebrow. I remember the summer I got it, and the winter I tried to burn it away with lasers. It will not budge, and I am grateful, because every morning I have to look at a part of myself I tried to wish into the air, and it reminds me of the very humanness of my cells.

———

My mother's recipe book is covered in a soft brown cloth that has worn out at the edges from being handled. It has letters down the side so you can find a neatly alphabetised recipe. In amongst the handwritten notes and cuttings from the paper stuck in with browning tape, we kids have written in pencil how we feel about different offerings in the book—the chocolate-chip biscuit recipe from America 'SO GOOD MUM!!!'—and tried out the crayon that has all the colours of the rainbow in it, crescents of yellow and red and blue and green curling in bright banners around my mother's words. She has written the names of the people she has got the recipes from in her beautiful writing that is all curves and swirls. It is a quiet living history, all of her young life as a wife and mother gathered in there. I have looked through it a hundred times, searching for recipes for corn fritters, and banana loaf, and Tex Mex dip, but I never noticed the page towards the back, which has a little list on it.

Egg
Margarine ½ teaspoon
Bread 1 slice

Tuna 60 grams
Salad

Fish 120 grams
Vegetables

It's a simple list, and it takes me some time to realise it is a diet plan of sorts, tucked away. I find it and I don't ask my mother about it, but consider when she would have implemented it, perhaps sometime between the arrival of my sister and me, or after the last of us came, and no more were planned, and she drew her body back into herself again. I see that quiet list and I feel the closest I have ever felt to my mother. I want to protect her. I feel her vulnerability, and her determination, and I feel the impact I have had on her body and identity. I am the human who came in and wreaked havoc, I am the reason she will never be the same.

Sometimes when we argue I think about that list, and it reminds me of the way I have taken her over, and it softens me and reminds me to be kind to her. The older I get, the more I relate to my mother on that page. I feel a kinship with her through my changing body, and a comfort in knowing she was there before me. As I seek out ways to liberate myself from the conventions I and others have inherited, and make a new frame of reference for the form I am taking up in this world, I feel her beside me. I begin to write a new history in careful handwriting just like hers.

Where I Walk

We are not allowed to pat the dogs, and my hands ache in the wanting. I see them coming before I see their owners, their tails happy flags in the grass, and I brace myself for the disappointment in their eyes as they rush to greet my knees and look up. They are down on their pat quotas and they know it. Their tails wag harder, begging for the touch that has been banished in this time. My whole body aches to rub their cheeks and run my fingers over their silky ears. I want to pat them good and firm on the flanks and see them quiver with happiness. I fold my arms behind my back and adopt a physical expression of respectful caution, so that the owners across the field can see I am not touching their dog. I see them tilt their heads in acknowledgement, and we walk on, criss-crossing hemispheres like diagrams of atoms in science class.

With every person I encounter it is the same: thin smiles, eyes glancing across the space between us, assessing the distance. One old man with his hands shoved deep in his pockets strides out over the school field and shouts at me as we cross paths, 'More than two metres! Much more!' and we smile at each other and give a desultory thumbs-up. Even our thumbs are failing us. They have much less to do now their jobs have been reduced. They can't find their place in the world when they do not form handshakes around other people's fingers.

The wind buffets rain in blousy sheets across the roads. The trees move like broken, half-hearted machinery. I walk and feel the tendons in my legs stretching, feel my blood move from my heart in routine circuits and the cool wind on my cheeks, and I know I am living in this strange day. I walk the track up Maungawhau from a suburban street and notice that building construction has ceased on several properties that have lately clattered with noise. The houses are wrapped in plastic, and security tape flutters in the breeze—the only movement except for the boughs of trees and the drizzle. At the top of the maunga the world seems still, the silver light flat and hard, the clouds close. There are barely any cars on the roads. I watch for minutes and see only two. The streets appear like a set, like something out of *Postman Pat*, and the cars come around the bend like little tokens of a real life. The blackbirds I often meet on these walks appear bolder, opportunistic, and they don't move out of my way as I walk by, but hold my gaze as if to level with me, as if to say: We are equals now on this Earth.

If I am still long enough, I can feel how this isolation we are all engaged in has registered with the Earth around us. There is a quietude and a space where before there was clutter, and I can almost hear the ground breathing as it takes the time to turn over, to reassess. On a track that takes me past a rope swing, I stop and wonder if I am going mad, because of the way I can discern life vibrating all around me, as if left alone just for a few days nature has increased its industry and pushed its aliveness out into the space we have occupied. As I walk, there is a strange euphoria in the day, a quiet one, a careful exultation of unhampered living.

At the primary school a man turns slow figure eights on his bike in the middle of the empty netball courts. His dog is a shaggy Alsatian with a dark head and caramel body, and he trots along beside the man in perfect time, his lead in a gentle loop attached to the handlebars. The man wears a PPE mask and his muffled voice calls out to me as I pass, 'Isn't it beautiful to be outside? Be safe, be well,' and he wheels away. The formality of his language reminds me of something I can't put my finger on. I wonder if it is Keats, with his romance and his flourishes. There is something in this turning autumn that is picked out in the man's words, and in the leaves his bike rides over.

On my way home I feel loneliness envelop me. I am the only person on the street, a ghost in track pants and messy hair. It's the street where I usually pick flowers that have poked their blooms out onto the footpath, but all the hedges have been trimmed now for autumn, and the wet trunks and twigs of the shrubs are like bones. Everything is bare. It's then I decide that I will leave messages for the people who walk the tracks of the maunga, in the world that breathes and is not online. I want to leave messages where it rains and the leaves fall and the tracks get slippery. I want to leave notes for the strangers I know will be out, grasping at the fresh air with their indoor bodies.

We keep trying for a baby, and I foster a hope I will get pregnant in lockdown and emerge in bloom, growing life. I tell myself it will make this time even more valuable. I can't access the medication and the monitoring that is the next step in our baby plan because the fertility clinic can't operate, but before I can stop myself I am mentally rearranging the spare room for a nursery. My sister says perhaps it's a good thing we do not succeed when things are so uncertain. But I want life to go on, to pin my hope to some new energy, though it's true—I don't know what our children are going to inherit.

Arun and I lie in bed and talk about our childhoods, and agree we got the best of it. We got unlimited dreams, and the thrill of plane rides without anxiety, and theme parks that never closed. We got jabs for rubella, endured chickenpox and eternal itching, and ran around unconcerned, our sores scabbing over. My biggest worries were whether the chewing gum would run out or I would miss seeing our monarch butterflies hatch. My nieces learn about viruses and stay home from school. They watch their father, a pilot, face potential unemployment. My brother's kids feel the tension of his worries in his small business that struggles, with his mortgage looming. My sister delivers groceries to Mum and stands on the drive to talk to her. My mother, worried for us kids and for her grandkids, cries.

I walk, and in the order of my feet moving in lines I find the impulse to keep going. I walk, and walk off my worry and frustration. I walk, and let my footfalls send messages to the ground.

I am still finding notes from my dad tucked away in biscuit tins (This is empty! Dad xx) and books (Dad was here xxx). He always left us notes, often ones pointing out that all the chips had been eaten or the baking had run out. Sometimes he'd just leave a note by your bed with a little drawing and his initials, and when you took it out to show him he'd smile, and you'd realise he'd left it for you weeks ago, just to let you know he was about. He once wrote his and my mother's initials on a tree on the track he knew I liked to walk through. He must have come down recently and written in Vivid marker on the trunk that leaned out beside the wooden boardwalk and mangroves. When I discovered it, I stopped and laughed, and it felt like magic. He grinned like a madman when I told him I had found it. I told him off for writing on a tree, but I loved it. The next time I walked there, the rain had washed the letters away and all that remained was the faint ghost of an L. I looked every time after that, just in case. His sloping capital letters, written in a rush. His words that always made me feel included, and seen.

The first note I leave says—

I hope you won't be too lonely

I write it on a piece of green plastic board, piercing the top with two holes to thread a bit of twine through. I tie it to the tree I always admire as I walk the track to the top of the maunga, and I leave it there. I hope nobody takes it down.

I have a dream I am walking up the maunga, along the track I usually take, up the path that curves around its base, a gradual upward spiral, past the rope swing and through the copses of trees until I hit the bitumen that bites into the side of the maunga like a scar. In my dream I recognise how vivid the landscape is. I can smell the damp leaves that crush beneath my feet. I tell myself I can't be dreaming if I am wondering about it, and just as I consider this I come across a baby lying in the leaves. The baby has no face that I recognise, its features smoothed into something you'd see on the 3D scan women get when they are pregnant. The curves of cheeks and the bump of a nose are there, but there are no eyes. Its nude limbs are sweetly plump. I pick it up and hold it to my jersey to keep it warm, and continue on my walk. I keep finding babies on the track, nestled in the grass or tucked up beside the trunks of trees. I can barely carry all the babies home with me, but somehow I manage. My husband and I try to bathe them, and wrap them up warm, but they keep shrinking and shrinking in our hands, until we are left holding the air in front of us.

I walk in the rain, in the soft showers that seem to fall every morning before clearing at noon, and feel the coolness on my tongue. I seldom encounter anybody, but when I do and I hear them talk, through the quiet their voices seem amplified, jarring. A woman shouts into her cellphone as she walks with a lopsided gait, and I learn about her son in quarantine in another country, and how she hasn't seen anybody on the road today. The notes of her rising inflection puncture the air, and I wince. I want to cover my ears.

I have adjusted so quickly to the quiet that I pick up every sound, and am sure I can hear the pops of air as earthworms come up from the wet soil. The first few nights of lockdown it took me a long time to fall asleep, the lack of sound was so acute. I thought about how it is often said that a silence is deafening, but now as I listen in the dark I notice how the silence lives inside itself, like a Russian doll, silence inside silence inside silence. My ears reach a quiet place, and then another is revealed, and another, and I travel down avenues of silence like it's a network, a road, a map. The rumble of the motorway has been muted. The city has reached a stillness I have never encountered before, and it seems as if we are the last people on Earth.

It's so quiet I can almost hear my heart beating—

is the next note I leave on the tree.

When I decided I would walk up the maunga every day during the lockdown, I hadn't anticipated the way I would drag my feelings with me from home and walk them up with me. I leave the house in a bad mood, my feet thumping on the concrete, sending waves of heaviness up into my hips. I have only just recovered from a tendon injury but push on anyway, as if making a point to the pavement.

Some days this walking feels futile. I don't know what I am looking for. I think I expect to reach the crater and see the world changed, but it's just as it was, quieter, less bossy, and I feel let down. I've never before looked for an epiphany when walking, so I don't know why I look for it now. I suppose I want solace in these feet that storm the footpaths, and slip on the loose rocks and dirt on the tracks. I'm lost, I think. I have lost a sense of time and of my function.

In the other room my husband works away, laughing with his colleagues on the phone and padding out into the kitchen to rustle for snacks. His familiar noises draw me back into the world. We will go on like this and it will never stop, I think. I track the day through the light that comes to flush the bedrooms with morning sun, or with a grey filter on wet days, and then moves in high arcs over our house before visiting again in the late afternoon. I lie in pools of light early and late, feel my skin meet the air and my molecules mingle with the hours that leave us.

Each day there are more and more swallows. At first I think I imagine it, but eventually I see other people seeing them and I know they are real. They skim through the air above the school fields, whistling close to the ground, their backs flashing royal blue. They are out to catch the insects we stir up with our feet, all these people out for constitutionals. There is something in the way they turn sharp curves in the air that reminds me of knives slashing. I remember them always being at the marina near our boat, picking up the bugs on the surface of the water, leaving tiny trails of their presence in the sea as they wheeled away. One winter they built a nest in the exhaust pipe of the boat. I think of Dad when I see them on the field, and indulge myself that the pair who fly close to me are the same pair we knew so well then, who flew around us each time we'd take the boat out, and would be there to greet us when we came back in.

I walk this field so much I wonder if I leave an imprint, if my form presses into the air, leaving the shape of me somewhere between the goalposts and the grass. The school-field ghost, out for a walk with the silence. I just walk and walk because I don't know what else to do, and because the walking gives me a sense of direction in a space that is otherwise devoid of it. I leave the house after our frequent fights—ones I start and am unable to finish—and I walk up the maunga to leave my offerings of bad-temperedness at the crater. The days start to melt and stick together, and my brain is gooey, so I check my body for the realness of my human form. I watch the food in the fridge diminish, and that's how I know I am here. When the day is over I open drawers and see that I have tidied them, I examine books newly arranged on the shelf, and I know that I am not a ghost.

I feel as if I am in a dream, and I miss being awake—

I write, and stick it on top of the other notes, securing it with tape from my pocket, watching over my shoulder for people coming up and down the track. On this day there is no one. I can't face the mountain today, so I walk back down and roam the streets, seeing my reflection in shop windows, hair shoved under a baseball cap, old tracksuit pants baggy around my bum. In the bookshop window a mannequin wears a face mask. The café beside it is dark, empty. I walk in the middle of a road where I often used to be held up in traffic. I walk through the main intersection where the lights are on their usual phasing, and I walk right through the red. It gives me no thrill. I miss all the people. I miss my family, who I usually see every week. I miss the hugs of the children who run to press their faces against my hip, and whose soft heads I pat and kiss. I miss the intimacy of hands.

———

This willingness to walk in all kinds of weather, to walk every day, to let my stride determine how I would go in the world, is not new to me. I have walked all my adult life, all over the world. I have walked when I have felt alone and isolated. I have walked when my life is too crowded and loud. I have walked to ease my heart, and to make fights with my own conscience. Every now and then I recall the way I had to be forced to walk as a child, and then especially as a teenager, when I'd growl and sulk furiously on walks with my family. It seems like a history belonging to someone other than me.

We used to anchor the boat off Waiheke, in the middle of summer after we'd been at sea for several weeks. We'd row ashore with our socks tucked into the sneakers tied around our necks by the shoelaces. On the beach we'd drag the dinghy up past the high-tide mark and sit down to rub the sand from our feet, before yanking on socks and tying laces, and setting off together, me bringing up the rear, a thundercloud on stick legs. In the high sun, on a dusty earth road and bits of rough track, we walked. It was usually Mum out the front, her tanned legs setting a swift pace, and my father behind her, often flanked by one of us kids, perhaps my brother, who took the time to whack the bushes with a stick he'd then pretend was a gun. My sister would be somewhere in there, fit, keen, laughing at our dad or remarking on the flowers by the trail.

The worst walk we ever did, the one that cemented my hatred for walks for years, was to Stony Batter, the old gun battery from the Second World War on Waiheke. I was thirteen then, and just beginning the phase where I loathed everything about being human, and especially walking, and most especially walking with my family. I wanted to stay on the boat and read my book, but I wasn't allowed. At some point in the walk I stopped like a stubborn donkey and hollered, 'I HATE THIS! I'M NOT WALKING ANYMORE!' I let the gap between my family and me stretch until they were up the hill and around a bend and gone from sight. The sun started to burn my nose, and the sand in my shoes started to itch. Nobody came back for me. The cicadas throbbed in the bushes at the side of the track, and I stood there for a long time. I looked up and down the road, and kicked the dusty gravel, and waited for someone to come back. Nobody came back. There wasn't any shade, and eventually I decided I'd just have to get on with it. Furious, overheated, my tongue sticking to the inside of my cheeks, I huffed after my family.

On that section of the walk, alone, I listened to my brain tell me everything I was incapable of. I listened to the way my thoughts chased and tumbled over each other like dogs at the beginning of a fight—with some kind of fast energy tinged with danger. The way of making it better was to keep walking and to tell myself that each step got me closer to my family, who I'd lately been so keen to be rid of. In the heat shimmer on the road ahead I thought I saw butterflies, but as I got closer it was only dust blown up into dervishes by the gusts of wind.

I dream with urgency about my mother's damaged lungs. I drive through the holes in them in a tiny car, up and up like I'm driving through a mountain pass, and the holes in her lungs become the tunnels I drive through to reach the peak. I worry about her lungs every night in my sleep, I see her coughing and pale, and I wake with sweat gluing my thighs together and my heart racing. Over FaceTime she brushes away any fears I have, tells me she is so bored she walked to the edge of the marina before she realised how far she'd gone, and had to hike home with a growling stomach. I look at her face, her mouth set in a firm line of stubbornness, and remember when she had pneumonia and I caught her vacuuming. I try to make her laugh, exaggerating stories of the silliness of our household trying to navigate a lack of personal space, and how Arun wears only undies and a tee-shirt to his work Zoom calls. She is missing Dad and the noisy way he filled the room, whistling and singing and calling her name for no reason, except he loved her. When we say goodbye she tells me that she loves me and to keep in touch, and her face is frozen in the frame before the call ends: her smile that is tight, her eyes that search mine.

It is one week since the country locked down, and a fine misty fog has settled around the house, and around the maunga. I walk through it, feeling fine droplets kiss my skin, and watch myself disappear into it like all those film montages where a character slowly vanishes into darkness, or down a lane, or into the sunset. I vanish into cotton wool, and let it embrace me. It is a while before I see anyone. People emerge through the thickness as ever-lightening shapes, the sound of their feet hushed by the cloak that has settled over the landscape. All the dogs have wet fur, and grass clinging to their paws and legs.

Up the maunga there is no view, except where tall buildings peep through the mist. An elderly man with heavy-rimmed glasses exclaims about how beautiful it is, and I agree, and we smile at the magic that only comes down in the fog. Omdifogdiron. I whisper to myself the made-up word from our childhood that means to play in the fog, and I feel the mischief of my dad come sidling up with a sideways grin.

'Omdifogdiron,' I say, a little more audibly. A woman has heard us talking and huffs past, her breathing laboured, her cheeks red as plums. 'Terrible view!' she complains as she stomps past. The man and I laugh, and I wind away down the road that leads to the track and down the path that widens into a little meadow where the swing I have swooped on so many times has been tucked into the branches of the tree. The clearing is barren, but the sun is starting to come though, and as the light hits the mist I see the particles twirling in the air, all dancing out of time with the day that is coming on. By the time

I hit the school field the fog has lifted and the sun is properly out, parading across the grounds. I run across the field and between the goalposts, lifting my arms in some kind of foolish victory. The truth is, along with the fog, something has lifted inside me.

I watch my moods rise and fall in sharp peaks and troughs like an electrocardiogram that is never switched off. I notice my laughter in short, staccato bursts, and then the silence where I begin to fret or watch the interior of my house for decay. On the national bulletin each day, the number of the dead begins to creep upward. I feel them like a punch and find myself mourning for strangers and for their families who cannot be with them. Compared to the rest of the world, our numbers are so low, only a few deaths, but every time someone comments on how lucky we are I think of those who have lost someone, the luck not extended to them, and how they must wish the person they loved and lost was not a statistic we pore over. I curl up in bed and watch the weather through the balcony door, and wait for the impulse to move.

When I go out to walk again I feel anxiety shaking the mainframe of my system like an earthquake underwater, all the feelings drifting upwards, dislodged. In the space of a day, a large number of journalists and writers have lost their jobs, and many magazines have filed their final copy. Overnight, all the best people are out of work, and it feels symbolic of a greater disease spreading. I notice that I walk leaning into the day, my torso tight. I am sharp lines against the blue sky and the high autumn light that is beaming regardless. It is the first time I have been afraid. I am afraid of the things we are losing, the words running away from us, the stories silenced. I am afraid for bank balances running low, and for the democracy generated in copy that will no longer go to print. I am afraid of the pain of those who lose family members. I am worried for everyone.

In my hand I clutch the rolled-up bit of paper with the latest note—

There are more birds in the day, and more stars at night

I don't know what else I can say. I am looking for signs of life in the natural world. I am looking for the animal kingdom that continues to thrive in our absence, and for the skies that seem less infected with industry, showing me constellations I can't usually spot from my little balcony in Epsom. I need to see something blooming, some benefit to the shrouded, shorter lives we are living. We sit out on the balcony at night with emergency cigarettes, and let the evening reassure us that another day will come. I speak the words of fear, and give them over to the inky dark, setting them free to run havoc where I can't see them, to be gone by sunrise. But I can't sleep, and the night seems endless.

I think I hear whispering when I leave the note. I tape it over the last one in haste, in case another person finds me here. I keep turning to look because I think I have been found, and the murmurs are disapproval. There is no one on the track, so I stop dead, my ears and eyes searching. It's a big clump of harakeke, the fronds rubbing against each other and smacking softly in the breeze that sounds like people talking. I stand there for ages, listening to what the harakeke has to say, and listening to the tūī whose songs are long ribbons of notes running like cool rivers across the morning. In the absence of people, and of technology that rings and clicks and beeps, the birdsong seems more old-fashioned, more analogue, unencumbered by artificial sounds. The birds have begun again.

I see that someone has tucked a sprig of blue flowers into a log where people often sit. From a distance I catch people taking photographs of the signs I have left. I feel the world, animal, vegetable, mineral, talking back to me. On the balcony of a house that backs onto the park, a family is taking a selfie. They have all shaved their heads, and their laughter rings out. I begin to see more people standing on their balconies, more people at windows. There are several places where I see the same elderly men and women at their windows, and I wave to them and they wave back. I want to show the days to them. I wonder if they come outside or not.

I watch for the deepening autumn, and find I am more connected to the world I can't spend much time in. I feel the subtle shifts in temperature acutely, feel the sun cartwheel across our roof in slow motion, watch the clouds moving fast and slow in the sky. Life has wound down to a crawl, and because of that I am awake to the tiny changes. The leaves start to turn and fall, and feijoas ripen on the trees that hang over the footpath where I walk. My cat has her winter suit on, and she's plush with it. After so many hours indoors, we all get confused by daylight saving, and wake up far too early and get cranky in the evenings. On the radio Kim Hill says someone has written in and said it's like being back in the 1950s, and it makes sense, matches up to the feeling I have that we are out of synch with our lives.

This is the most beautiful autumn I have ever seen—

I write for the tree, and leave it, and walk up the mountain where the views extend in perfect clarity. Every morning now is still, the vault of the sky blue and endless. There is still warmth in the sun, though the evenings are cool. It is relentlessly beautiful. But I feel tired with the days that seem to repeat and recycle, with nothing to differentiate them except the number of cases of the virus, deaths and job losses. My legs are heavy from walking. My eyes are tired from trying to find positive ways of seeing things. My niece has her sixth birthday, and we sing over a group chat and she beams. We all keep talking over each other, and the images break up and the sound distorts. I exit the chat early and lie down, feeling thin on my insides. I call my mother later and she's down too, and I don't know how to pick her up. We have reached a flattening out, but not of infection, of enthusiasm.

We start sleepwalking. Arun wakes up to find he has left his mouth guard on the kitchen bench during the night. I wake to find my bottles of vitamins and some hair ties have migrated to the living room. Once in the night I move my handbag and coat from their hooks to the couch. We sleep heavily, but in our sleep we are moving all the time, trying to work the anxiety out in our dreams, trailing it through the night via bodies which toss and turn and wake up and garble new words. I wake to Arun on his hands and knees in the bed, a hulking dark form on a darker night. I try to help him back to sleep, but he resists, heavy and solid like a sleeping horse in a field. I go into the spare room where the sheets are cool and where the streetlights pool through thinner curtains.

In our nights we are restless. In all of my dreams I am active: I search for something; I find and collect; I try to protect. When the light starts to come up in the morning I feel relief, and cling to the changing colours of dawn, watching the darkness withdraw from the sky like sheets pulled back from a bed. There is certainty to daylight hours.

At Easter I drive to see my mother, take her groceries, ice creams and fresh watermelon. She's alone in lockdown, and missing us all. Like me, she has taken to walking several hours each day just to move and to keep her mind off her grandchildren, and away from the worry she has about us kids and how we will manage now work is leaving us. In the car on the way over I cruise in a solo line down empty sections of motorway. On the radio a doctor in America is talking about bunkers and the end of the world. He says there are women in Tennessee living off the grid, repairing things, preparing for the apocalypse and learning crafts. I wish I had bought wool before we all tucked ourselves away. I could have made scarves for everyone. Scarves in bright colours and extra-long for winding round our necks when we emerge. I could have asked Mum to teach me how to knit a jersey over Skype.

The relief at seeing my mother's face and hearing her voice in the same atmosphere as my own takes my breath away. We sit on either side of the glass doors of her patio and steal ten minutes to talk. We have no news, and that in itself is a novelty, because we haven't been anywhere and nothing much has happened. Instead we tell each other about our walks and the things we see—on hers, people arguing about swimming and distance on the promenade, yelling and swearing at each other and calling the police; on mine, all the dogs I can't pat, and the birds I encounter, so many of them. I look at her garden, which has grown so much since I was last there, and pinch some of her parsley, and we make plans for what we will buy when the garden centres are open.

The way we talk about what we will do when lockdown is over is like the way people mythologise other centuries for their greatness. The things we want are simple, though:

human company, the comfort of family, the reassurance of old routines returning.

I don't want to say goodbye. I want to curl up on her couch and read my book and listen to our old cat yowling. I want to cook food with her, play Rummikub and laugh. When I go to leave, we stand on either side of her ranch slider and mime hugs, wrapping our arms around the air, burying our faces in the gaps where our bodies should be. I tell her to just keep walking. 'You walk and I will,' I say. I remember how she always used to apologise that I had inherited her legs, which she claimed were bandy, a bit scrawny, with no shape to their calves. They're strong legs, though, legs of a packhorse used to pacing and carting and travelling. These are the legs walking in unison with mine, in different parts of the same town, working it out through the movement, carrying on, because the only thing you can do is put one foot in front of the other.

My friend who has anxiety the way I do tells me that for the first time in a long time she feels calm. It's like the whole world has come down to my level, she says. Everyone is anxious, and trying to find structure and routine in an existence changing daily, so she is not alone. The routines she keeps to feel normal are the routines of us all now, and there is peace in that. We form our days around when to work, when to shop and prepare food, and when to take a walk or a bike ride or run. People with children make room to teach. At some point we all go to sleep, and then we wake up again. Online I see people talking about the wildness of their dreams and I realise that nothing I am dreaming is unique, except that it is tailored by my unconscious, a thick cloak containing the secrets of my brain, wrapping me up in surprises at night.

I hope we can hold on to some of this simplicity—

is my final note. The rain has bled through them all, sending Vivid marker streaming in runnels. All the words are wet together, the meanings belonging to each other—a wet history of these weeks. I wind tape around and around the damp card to hold it. The wind lifts its edges and makes it flutter in the tree as the rain comes down.

—

The clouds race on a Friday morning when I set out to walk under heavy grey skies. On the school field a dad is laying a kite out along the grass, the bright-coloured tail ribbons lifting away from the string as if trying to launch themselves. He picks up the orange body of the kite, calling to his young son to run. The little boy's name is Bruno, and he waits for the second RUN before he trots off, his chubby legs going fast beneath his sturdy torso. The wind collects the kite as if it has been waiting for it, and lifts it up in a sudden jolt, launching it high in the air. The dad whoops, and I watch as Bruno runs and runs.

The kite is higher than the classrooms, but Bruno doesn't look up to watch it, he's so focused on his job as the runner. He starts to curve to the left, flanking the side of a prefab, and I watch his dad recognise what is about to happen. He yells out 'Stop, Bruno, come back!', as I yell out 'Oh no!', and the kite hits the treeline and thumps onto the roof of the classroom. Back comes Bruno, with flushed cheeks, running as fast as he can with the string in his fist, until it snags and stops him in his tracks. Everyone out on the field stops for a moment and watches the dad show him the kite on the roof, and how his small face falls. We are united in this most simple pursuit. We're all Bruno, doing our best, and we're all that kite, sometimes airborne, sometimes stuck.

The weeks yawn, but there are guavas on the tree again down the road, and I stuff my raincoat pockets with them, interrupting my walk to chew on them, their perfumed seeds getting stuck in my teeth. The roads are thick with fallen leaves, and the rain is intermittent, bringing the damper, cold autumn with it. We buy hot-water bottles and slippers online, and when we hear the feet of the delivery man on the stairs we're excited by the break in our day. We shuffle around in slipper boots that are the wrong size because we couldn't try them on, and scare the cat, who is used to our light footfalls in the house.

We are moving to Level 3 shortly, and my husband and I decide to merge our bubble with his family, so we can be close to his grandmother, whose health has declined in recent weeks. My mother makes plans to join my sister's bubble and is more cheerful when I talk to her.

I visit the maunga on Anzac weekend. It heaves with

visitors, and feels too loud, too disruptive. So often I have to climb up on the banks to wait for people to pass, the track feels like a highway and I go back home. Instead, I walk the streets each day as if to re-introduce myself to other humans, walking Dominion Road, past all the shuttered shops, and Potters Park, which is still, unloved by children and dogs. I feel myself coming back into the world after a period of absence. My walks up Maungawhau have kept me shielded from industry, but now I am ready to be part of a busy city again.

In the evenings we make dinner and our conversations turn to daydreaming. We say things like 'When this is over I will . . .' Like the story starters we used in the primers, we tell each other tales of what we will do when lockdown is lifted. It starts with driving to the beach, and shared family dinners. We dream of having friends over to play the board game which has taken six weeks to arrive. Normal things like being able to buy seedlings at the plant centre, and good new soil so I can get my winter balcony garden up and away before it's too late. But then it moves to the philosophical, to the things we have learned and want to change—not buying so much unnecessary stuff, finding delight in tiny things, appreciating our families more. We say we will be more thoughtful about our creativity, and make more time in the day for books and words and art. In this time locked away we have found new rhythms of work, and vow to hold them for as long as we can. We don't need as many things as we thought. We just need each other, and our families and friends. When this is over, we say, we won't take so many things for granted.

On the last day of lockdown Level 4, I walk around my neighbourhood and make an effort to say hello to as many people as I can. Their faces are alight with the small liberties approaching, and we share the kind of smiles you make when something better is coming. These five weeks tucked away have brought strangers closer. I wonder how long it will take for us all to snap back into old ways of being, like rubber bands set free. I hope I will remember the way these days slowed down to show me things, to allow time to sit with the spaces inside me. I want to keep the quiet of these days close, and look for myself imprinted on the landscape where I walk.

Rabbits

The first whole sentence I wrote in primary school was 'Jane Beatson is my best friend.' I wrote it at the end of my first week, faithfully copying my teacher's felt-tip pen example on the line above. She must have thought it was sweet or funny, because she showed it to Jane Beatson's mother after school, and Jane Beatson's mother looked at me and laughed. I had only just met Jane Beatson and she wasn't my best friend at all, but I hoped she would be. I hoped it so much that my small hands wrote it out, as if doing so might conjure that friendship from the air, as if those painful letters, heavy with lead and pressed with method, might make her mine.

Several years later, at dinner at Jane Beatson's house, when I was about eight and she still wasn't my best friend, her mother brought up that day and laughed about it again. She was the kind of mother whose manner made it hard to tell if she was being unkind or not. Plump with the heat, and wearing those short-sleeved cotton shirts which clung to her bosom, she always seemed rosy and flushed with colour as she moved around the house. It was confusing to think that someone so tidy—she reminded me of a Sylvanian Family figurine—might be unkind, but her demeanour and her words didn't always match, and I was a bit afraid of her.

I suppose a five-year-old child declaring a best friend in writing after five days at school might have seemed intense. It's possible Mrs Beatson didn't like the tone of possessiveness with which I appeared to claim her child. Perhaps she thought I was mad, this little blonde thing whom she hadn't been able to get rid of. I took dance class each week with her daughter, and most weeks I came after school to eat a chocolate digestive and watch the television until it was time to go. Some days we would make Five Cup biscuits in the kitchen and eat them hot out of the oven, the raisins boiling on our tongues. Because my parents were fastidious about manners, I was very polite and anxious to be on my best behaviour, and said please and thank you and excuse-me-may-I, and perhaps that's what annoyed her about me. Once at the dinner table she made fun of my manners to her husband. 'Oh, there we are—excuse me please!' and a little tinkling laugh at the end to lighten the derision.

Children are not stupid. It was clear to me that she

thought I was obnoxious, and had done so since that first week of school. Because you are small, nobody has taught you how to manage the crushing blow of unpopularity. You have no armour, young as you are with your new flesh and loose body, and you haven't needed any, sheltered in the shade of your family. Just on mathematics alone, stepping into a school means navigating hundreds of new people all the time: someone is bound not to like you. In the case of Mrs Beatson, she became one of the women I feared the girls in my class would grow up to be like, and I was scared of her, and them, all through my childhood.

I had absorbed the dream of a best friend from when I was very young. My sister and I were *Anne of Green Gables* fanatics, and the idea of a bosom friend gripped us as soon as we saw the movie. Anne and Diana were kindred souls, bound in friendship forever. Even before that, so many books, like *Frog and Toad are Friends*, made me long for someone to write me a letter and tell me they were glad I was their best friend. That was probably where I got the idea to write about Jane Beatson in the first place.

It was imprinted on us that from the moment we began to separate from the family group into our own individual suns that we would find a moon to shine our light on, and be a moon for someone else. It was the rite of passage we experienced before puberty; it carried as much importance as getting your period—having a best person in your corner, and someone to invent the world with. You marked your ground and claimed space with your friend, and that's how the world framed up from there, always from the point of view of two. For someone as shy as I was, a two was imperative. Two meant a voice for me if I fell silent, two meant someone to always play Snap! with, two meant a friend complicit in make-believe. I ached for a two, and faced the terror of primary school, and total strangers, with the tremulous but naïve certainty that I would find my best friend, walk hand in hand with her to the library and share sandwiches with her at lunchtime.

It's brutal when children have their hopes shattered. I met Jane Beatson and decided she was the one, but her mother thought otherwise and most likely her daughter did too. Jane Beatson had the sturdy constitution that attracted others like ants to a dropped ice cream. She was robust, she was fearless on the jungle gym, and she had shiny long hair, neither thick nor thin and perfectly straight. She had just the right amount of silliness for a girl, capable of cantering off round the field pretending to be a horse, and you'd never see her crying, only cheerful or concentrating. I attached myself to her, a happy moon, but already anxious, always checking and double-checking that I wasn't doing anything wrong. I think that's where the concept of love or caring running out first wormed its way under my skin. I couldn't keep pace with the way kids around me changed each day—it seemed so volatile, the way allegiances shifted in the space of a morning playtime or on the way home from school, so that the next day you'd find yourself in the playground alone.

I grew, and stretched away from those agonising years, but freedom came with invisible tethers. A people-pleaser, I put myself at a disadvantage to make others happy. I spent so much time moulding myself into the versions of me that I thought people wanted, I couldn't make out my true form in the mess. It's possible that's why acting came to me so easily—slipping into the skin of the characters I played in my own life became my second nature.

My sister and brother were confident children, and I'll never know why I failed to inherit that quality. Some people just seem to exist in the world with a good strong assurance of their place, and I envy them. Our parents did their best to build in us a robust stoicism, but while I could endure difficulty, I didn't thrive. Shy, gangly and adrift, I migrated between groups of friends, while my siblings were pressed into noisy throngs like happy sprats in a shoal. I liked my own company, but it was a learned enjoyment and something I accepted as a default prize by virtue of not having a best friend, and of being scared of talking to people in case I got rejected. I never seemed to land anywhere, and being an interloper was lonely.

The first time my niece came home from school with swollen cheeks and a forced smile going nowhere, I felt such pain for her that I lost any ability to comfort her. As she spoke about a girl who didn't want to play with her anymore, a wave of shame and fear coursed through me as if it were happening to me again. She was five-and-a-half and I would have snapped the world in two if I could, if it would have helped her to feel better.

I held her little body to me and told her that there were lots of other kids to play with and she had many friends and she was a good, kind kid, and fun to be with. I hoped it was enough, even as I felt the words slide off the air in front of my mouth and vanish. She nodded her head in an automatic gesture, because even so young she had learned that it was my role to reassure her. I hoped the hurt would glance off her and she would forget, hoped her sweet and kind spirit would bounce away like a rabbit in the grass and she would recover, but I lost hours worrying she wouldn't. I wanted to go into school and find the girl and ask her why she had been so unkind. I wanted to go back to my own school and ask the same question of the kids I had played with, as if understanding the cruelty could set my past to rights and protect my niece's future.

In my twenties I went to a healer. I was looking for a sense of belonging that I didn't feel in my pedestrian life on Earth. I wanted to feel connected to the bigger nature, to lift out of my loneliness and go wider. The healer told me that contrary to the generally accepted wisdom of development, we come into the world as babies with fully formed spirits and personalities, and everything we are, in our truest expression, is already with us. After that we just grow into our bodies and let the experience of life nudge up against us. I still wonder about this. There was nothing in my upbringing to plant the seeds of vulnerability that are part of my earliest memories. I don't remember a time where an anxious little current didn't run beneath the happiness of my everyday existence. I think I did just come in that way, in the same way that my niece arrived with a sweet spirit and gentle nature, and her younger sister arrived like a bomb exploding, shaking the world around her with her particular, unleashed energy.

I talk to my friends about this, and we piece together our histories, noticing the way they match one another. I find relief in the stories that seem to line up to my own, and can see how my tiny battles didn't happen in isolation. We examine the words that were said to us in forensic detail, turning them over to try to make sense of the motives behind them. In the end, the only conclusion is that all children must feel some kind of worry about belonging, and so we exact these cruelties not out of spite but out of a need to protect ourselves from the slights we sense are coming. Though I remember only the stinging pain of rejection, I'm sure I said unkind things to other children too. Perhaps I did that so I could have some control and not feel I was being lobbed around from group to group like a ball everyone had lost interest in playing with. Maybe we just passed the unkindness on, like in a game of pass the parcel, and everyone took a turn to hold the paper-wrapped prize of exclusion.

At five you are so optimistic about the world. If you are fortunate, as we were, nothing bad has happened to you. Life is mostly about begging permission to go on the trampoline after dinner, and whether you really have to wash your hair or it can wait another night if your mum French plaits it so it's tidy. In our street, all the kids played together. We played Spotlight, shared trampolines and fireworks in November, rode bikes round the cul-de-sac; nothing was really organised by age or gender. We were simply in the kid business. I had no idea about the subtle negotiations at work in a school playground.

Our primary school had a Girls' Hill which was a section of land with a sloping hill up one end and some big trees down the bottom. Boys weren't allowed to play on Girls' Hill. You'd see them chucking balls around the perimeter and occasionally losing one to the soft grass of our private oasis, and then negotiations would begin about who would throw the ball back. It seemed complicated and a kind of trickery. It othered us, made us separate. Some days I wanted to run with the boys, pounding the asphalt in a serious game of chase; other days I wanted to sit under a tree and pretend it was enchanted. But if you'd crossed a line and been seen playing with the boys, you were an outcast. You had boy germs, you had fraternised with the enemy, rumours might start about you not having any friends except boys. I walked the tension of wanting the wrong things, and I felt it all the time. Home was freedom, a place where we could all run together in a herd of exuberance, like cattle escaped from a paddock.

Once I sat on the barbecue table next to my dad while we watched the rubbish burn in the old metal bin that sat in the garden. I wasn't very old—perhaps six or seven. I don't remember how the subject of friends came up, but I remember going silent, and feeling ashamed. I had them, they existed, but not a best friend yet, and I said so. I couldn't really see Dad's face, but I remember what he said because of the way it made me feel. 'Your mum and dad are your best friends. We're the best friends you'll ever have, Mouse. I promise you that. You've got us for life.' My throat ached, and we watched the ash from the fire spin across the air in bursts of grey confetti, and I felt his big hand pat my back, and was grateful—but also worried.

That time was so full of the wonder of learning, and of the terror of being the wrong kind of kid. Learning to write seemed the most powerful thing imaginable, and as I hunched over my paper I felt the world come alive in a new way now that I could record it. I moved from pencil to pen, linked up my letters, and felt the force of the words under my fingers even as I felt the force of the words we all said to each other.

I don't want to play with you anymore.

Go and play with the boys.

This is my new best friend.

I couldn't keep up with the shifts and turns of the friendships and failures that seemed to spin on an ever-changing wheel, stopping each day at a different place. I became an interloper, accepting I was never on the inner circle of friendships but grateful to be included. I must have been about eight when the words always coming out of my mouth were 'What's this?' as I'd come up to a group of girls and try to make myself part of their conversation, standing there keen and eager, hoping to be thrown a bit of the subject to chew on.

It was always like that. I tried so hard to be liked, and to do the right things. My mother organised play dates, and kids would come and we'd play with the toys at my house, and it all seemed fine, except I had separated out from my body and was hovering somewhere in the space above us, watching anxiously as the afternoon unfolded, hoping everything was right, and this kid on the floor of our rumpus room would go to school the next day and report on a nice afternoon. You absolutely cannot live like that as a child, so it's not any wonder I became two versions of myself in the world: Michelle at home and running barefoot, or climbing trees, or jumping elastics, or down at the creek, and Michelle at school, in a meek kingdom, observant and worried. If you look at the faces of kids in their annual school photos you can see it in some of them—the hope and the strain.

I turned eleven. I was tall and thin, and wore glasses for the first time. I mostly walked with my head down to take away from my height, and because to make eye contact with other students would have set me ablaze with embarrassment. There was no family allegiance at intermediate, and I found that out fast; I had foolishly traded on the misplaced notion that because my cousin mixed with a group of girls in my class, I might be able to join them. When I asked one of them if I could play too, she looked at me, her bright blonde hair catching the sun, leaned on one hip and said, 'We don't *play*, we hang out.'

She said it plainly, with only a moderate trace of scorn, but the words held knives because they told me I had misunderstood everything. I didn't have any currency and I was out of date. Of course these girls didn't play anymore. They sauntered across the field with their socks up to their mid calves and their black school shoes thoughtfully scuffed. Their uniforms were short, but nobody minded because they'd be leaving intermediate soon and there was no point getting new ones. You could always tell a Form Two girl because you could see where her mum had let the skirt hem down to the last millimetre, leaving creases that never quite ironed out.

I felt the determined shift over that time, as we all moved away from our soft colonies of discovery and adventure, and hardened into communities built more around status and development. More than ever we began to feel the separation between boys and girls. Our puberty came crashing in like a drunk person, stumbling through, knocking everything down, even friendships.

I managed to tag along with a group of about six girls in my class, and though they were casual friendships they protected me from being alone at interval. Boys became the subject of every lunchtime discussion, of every note passed between the rows of desks. We called Mondays 'baking days' when the bravest of us would go to the edge of the field where it met a track, and kiss a boy of our liking. One by one the girls in my group 'went round' with a boy, and one by one on baking day they'd learn how to kiss in the clutch of heavy trees and shrubs at the edge of the school.

I never did. I succumbed to shyness, and to the fear of the public ritual, and froze. With my glasses and gangly frame, I was not a natural choice for a girlfriend, and I didn't have the easy confidence of the others. I focused on my schoolwork, and reading, and built an inner life to which I retreated when I couldn't stretch to the places my friends were, shiny with popularity and smooth with the gloss of confidence. In cars, on drives to hot pools, all of us crammed into the back seat and the boot, singing along to tapes we had made of the top songs off the radio, I sang with abandon—until one of my friends told me off for singing loudly. I wasn't quite right, ever, and sometimes I'd sit in the front seat with the adult who was driving and feel myself out of time with everyone. When we left intermediate, my friends were going off to a different high school. I had never kissed anyone, I didn't sing in public anymore, and I faced the next part of my education alone.

There is nothing like the sickening fear of new places. I walked to high school on the first day with a body full of hot rocks heating me up from the core, so I arrived sweating, worried, acutely aware that the brand-new bag on my back was too clean. I had fought with my mother over being allowed a new bag, and fought with her again over my school shoes, begging for her to buy the black ones with the yellow stitching which cost more but made up for it by granting instant access to acceptance. The shoes I ended up with were like wide black paddles. I scraped them on the curb outside our house to scuff them, and walked through dusty grasses to try to take the shine off them. Nothing worked. I may as well have carried a banner announcing my status as the most feeble person at college.

On my first walk across the school field between classes I was hit on the head by a rugby ball. It knocked my ponytail sideways and my heart into my ankles. It felt like an omen, but became an emblem for the lurching way I navigated my life in that school—with a thumping heart and cringing humiliation. Most of us were strangers on that first day in class, and we all made shy attempts at friendships, but I was wary. It seemed so forced and so difficult. I watched the kids the way dogs at the SPCA watch people taking home other dogs: I waited to be chosen, to be taken home by friends, and in that torturous wait I lost myself. Every time I had to walk into our common room alone I died a little inside, and after two weeks felt myself a lanky ghost half-dead with nerves. So I latched on where I could and made the best of it. But then it went wrong.

What is most insidious about bullying is the way it eats you up on the inside, like a chest of drawers chewed out by borer. You look like yourself, but your interior is a palace of decay, undermined a little more each day by the words and actions that eat at your self-esteem, making you hollow. I wonder if it's worse when it comes from the people you think are your friends. It happens so subtly you can't be sure if you're imagining it, and then before you know it you're isolated and confused. I wonder if it's even worse when you've been a participant in your own demise by being easily led to say and do things that aren't in your nature, to fit in with your group.

Over about a year, the tentacles of other kids, and not kind ones, began to wrap around me. They were girls on the periphery in my classes, brassy, strong and entitled, and because I was always trying to make friends, I let them in. I went away to school in America for half a year, and by the time I returned these girls were the only ones left to hang out with. They had quietly worked to separate me out from the first friends I had made. I didn't know that the letters I'd written to them were shared around, that the stupid things I had said, agreeing with them about other girls, half-heartedly, and from a homesick world in another hemisphere, would be the knives that bled me dry.

The first time I walked into my form room after that

period overseas, none of the nice girls I had liked and been loose friends with would look at me. Then someone told me what had happened. There followed my first-ever panic attack—in the toilet block beside our common room. Fluorescent with heat and shame, I crouched on the floor and tried to find air to breathe. I wanted to run from the school and never return. I saw the next three years stretching ahead as an endless loop of mistakes and isolation. I had no concept of moments passing. I was in the jaws of a terrible animal, and knew it was my own fault. I went into the sick bay and I said I didn't feel well, and I was so upset the lady there let me go home.

My mother was silent as she drove me home, and I didn't know how to tell her what had happened. I felt sure I would be blamed, and I already blamed myself. I was worried she would be angry, that her silence meant she would ignore me too. I begged to change schools. Over several weeks I executed a campaign of wheedling, bribing and outright threats. I yelled when I was woken up for school, I cried, I couldn't eat. My parents didn't budge. I must have been a mystery to them, this girl they barely recognised, all sharp edges and shouting. Anxiety cleaved a space between my parents and me, and it was a distance they couldn't reach across, and one I desperately wanted to traverse but couldn't. Each day repeated itself in fits of rage and tears and panic, and each afternoon I came home silent.

I think of the casual ways we all hurt each other in

school, and wish I could send messages back across my history to the younger me who was so miserable to reassure her things would change. At the time it was so consuming. It felt like the whole world existed in that school, down to the most microscopic life, the feelings swarming like bacteria on a petri dish. I negotiated with my parents that if I could get into university early, they would allow me to go. I managed it, but not before I'd endured two years of a bleak kind of misery, where I had my work stolen in the weeks before exams, where the girls I had trusted made fun of me within earshot. Through sheer luck, some kids I went to drama with let me join their lunchtime dance group. We would escape into a lecture room to listen to The Cure, and look at art, and very occasionally move our bodies around the space. It got me through, kept me steady enough to survive, and I was grateful. I left school at sixteen.

I hoped that university and my adult life would bring freedom from the anxiety I tried to keep tamped down, but I found the patterns repeating all through my early adulthood. The imprints made on a young spirit endure, and though the situations change the feelings do not. I will always reckon with belonging, I will always fear exclusion, and though time has made me kinder to myself, and given me clarity about human behaviour, it is still the little worry that makes a new nest somewhere in my body each year of my life.

On a summer afternoon, twenty years later, I left my house to walk through the muggy heat to the bottle store up the road from my flat. It was warm around the edges of everything, and I didn't have much to do but go out for cold wine to have with dinner. Up ahead of me a car pulled close to the curb and a woman got out. She hovered by the boot and kept glancing at me. I got closer and she called out my name, stepping onto the pavement, asking if I remembered her. Something in her face was familiar, but I apologised and said I couldn't really tell because of her sunglasses. She removed them and said her name. It was one of the girls from high school who had made life very hard. My body tensed and got stringy immediately, as if my muscles and tendons had started to separate, and I felt the urgent need to go to the toilet.

She evaluated me with the same gaze I remembered—eyes that moved quickly across me, and a half-smile that showed her even teeth and her pink tongue. She asked how I was, and I was careful and told her I was well. I couldn't ask it back, I could barely speak, and I didn't know if she had pulled over expressly to speak to me or just happened to be stopping there as I came by. I could smell my winter school jersey in my nostrils, and my hands reached down for my school skirt, to grope for the hem I wanted to turn in my fingers. Her voice halting, she began in the middle of an idea about our high school, and then doubled back around to tell me she had thought about me a lot over the years. She was monitoring me to see what I would give away in my body. Maybe she hoped to see nothing—no pain and no recollection—but I told her I remembered how it had been, and she began to cry. She said she felt so badly for the way she had treated me and had thought about it as she followed my career over the years. I couldn't feel anything except a peculiar buzzing in my ears, and my arms betrayed me and I hugged her. I heard myself tell her that high school was an unkind place and we were all probably unkind to each other, even though I didn't really believe it. I told her I was glad it was over. And then I said goodbye.

I moved away like a sleepwalker. At the liquor store I chose wine and handed over money. I went home and opened the bottle and sat on my bed and drank glass after glass. It was not an easy relief that spread through me. In my veins I felt validation and trouble. Somewhere I had been complicit in the easing of a guilt, and I wasn't sure I wanted that. I wanted the validation of my time at school to come without the deliverance of compassion to the person who harmed me, but I had been unable to remain impassive, unable to punish. All the words I had saved up like sharp teeth had nothing to bite into. These useless, decades-old fangs just had to be put away, because in the forgiveness I had given away my fight.

The imagined reckonings never arrive like they do in film clips. There are no killer lines delivered with devastating accuracy. You do not wear the kind of considered and dazzling wardrobe that sets you apart. Your fringe does not fall in your eyes just so, just carelessly cool. You don't get to walk away with an upbeat song stirring beneath your footsteps, growing louder as the credits roll. Instead you are there in limp living colour, your unwashed hair, your old jeans, just standing there hoping for the best the way you always have. You listen with your heart in spite of everything, and seeing someone's pain is enough to allow you to let it go. You let it all go now, and that is how you know you are grown. You let it go, and for the first time your young and old selves catch up to each other, and bounce away like rabbits in the grass.

Love Like This

On the cassette tape my grandfather's voice is all soft burr and lilt of Scotland. He says hello to my aunt, and sends his best wishes, and falls silent as we kids take over, my sister yelling out about punching noses, my mother telling her off, my timid voice singing a song. We passed the tape back and forth across hemispheres, sending it to California alongside the Christmas presents and sweets, and cards we had made for our cousins, and getting it back at Easter, with new messages and decals to decorate eggs, and American chocolate. I used to listen to Uncle Alec say Merry Christmas in his beautiful Scottish accent, and try to remember him. I used to make up the things he liked—whiskey (my mother silent) and lollies, at which she smiled, because the only real memory I have of him is visiting his little unit at the care home, where he had hung bags of Empire lollies from the curtain hooks above his hospital bed. He let us choose a bag to take home and share, and we would fight over which to choose but always end up with acid drops, or boiled sweets with flowers in their centres. I remember his cough, which started deep in his lungs and cleared a way to his throat as if it were an actor making a dramatic entrance. Then we would pause to listen, and watch his chest heaving, and hear the pull and drag of his breath. I think he had emphysema. I don't like to ask my mother how he died, though I know it was related to smoking and drink.

I have never asked her why we called him Uncle Alec instead of Grandad, because it seems so private, her upbringing with him and with her mother who died of alcohol-induced problems well before we were born. Instead I would take the tin box with all her photographs in, and pore over the images of my grandparents and make my own mythology about them. Like why my grandmother had formal photographs taken dressed as a man, smoking a cigarette with insouciance. Her gaze on the camera held mirth and disdain. She was unreachable. Someone told me she went on a boat to Japan and modelled as a man for some time. No reason was given. They exist in my fabrications, Estelle and Alec, as two alcoholics in a war with themselves, their children the casualties. I piece them together through the rumours that run in my small family; I see my mother walking my grandmother to get her wrist taped at the doctor and telling him my grandmother fell down the stairs, instead of being pushed from a stool by Uncle Alec. At Christmas I always think of the year they had no presents, when Uncle Alec crashed his truck, blind drunk on his way home, and all their Christmas money went into repairs. These were my grandparents, though they were never mine at all. When I was young, my mother spoke more about her own grandmother, a woman she loved and who loved her back. She told us stories of the baking her grandmother did, and her warmth and good humour. In photographs in the tin box the little woman has a mischievous grin, wire spectacles, and hair pinned in curls to her head. She is both stern and jolly. She looks like my mother, and squints into the camera the way my mother squints: a little unsure, but with warmth at the ready.

Dad's recollections were rough and brushed over. My grandfather a bully and a gambler, vanishing when Dad was small, never to reappear, never to father him, much less grandfather me. He wasn't even alive when I was born. I am no part of him at all, but I have inherited Dad's hurt at his mistreatment, and it has shaped the way I became alert to injustice from a young age, leaping to defend and protect my feelings, and everyone else's. His own grandparents had bigger things to worry about, Frank a politician in the first Labour Government, and Molly, his wife, who supported him. Molly was still alive when I was a child, and we'd go to see her, and wind up the canary in the metal cage on her mantelpiece and listen to its fluting song, and eat jubes and biscuits. Molly had the energy of at least three people, and she'd talk about politics and warn my mother about the meanness of the men in our family once drink was on board. She was sparkly, brash and funny, and forthright with her opinions about everything, even her marriage. Frank didn't sound like much of a grandfather at all: a great orator, but a bit of an asshole, it was agreed. Aside from getting nasty when drinking gin, which got banned from our house by my mother, Dad managed to escape most of the predilections of his forebears and rewrite history for us kids. He was the dad he never had and the protector he had always craved.

By the time I was three-and-a-half, our only grandparent was my dad's mum, and she was developing Alzheimer's disease, and fading out of life just as she began to fade out of our family gatherings, her attention in some other sphere, her gaze with her memories. My parents felt the loss keenly, and they took out a small advertisement in the local circular, asking if there was an elderly couple living in the Howick and Pakuranga area who might like to adopt three children as their grandkids. The only people who answered the ad were an English couple, newly arrived in New Zealand, where they had grown-up children. They lived in a little unit about a three-minute drive from our place. I am not sure which is more unusual, to advertise for extra grandparents or to answer the ad, but the couple who came into our lives became part of our family overnight, filling in the shapes of the older figures we needed, and solidifying the mystique and power of the grandparent forever.

Their names were Blanche and Fred. They had soft accents and they read us bedtime stories, the waltz of their English accents adding magic to the narratives. They made us ham sandwiches, and taught us how to play dominoes in their sunlit sitting room with photographs on the sideboard and net curtains looking out into a little concrete cul-de-sac. At our place we enticed them into games that involved building pillow forts and shooting Nerf guns down the hallway, yelling and screaming. They would have been in their mid sixties then, but they were down on their hands and knees, right in the game, lethal shots and more patient than us, buying time until they could make an accurate shot at whoever had been chosen to run up the hall in a dash for freedom. We accepted them without a moment's thought, all three of us. They were ours, and they came over almost every week, and they came for birthdays and for festive occasions, except Christmas. We begged them to join us on Christmas Day, but they never did—that day was for their own children and grandchildren. On birthdays they came with a card and ten or twenty dollars tucked inside—an enormous amount when I was small. I bought my first cassette tape with that money. It was Bryan Adams' *Reckless*.

Blanche, whom we called by her surname Massey,

because we couldn't pronounce Blanche, wore blouses tucked into skirts, and a gold locket that rested on a fine chain just below her throat. I sat on her lap and asked to open it every time I saw her. My little fingers handled the clasp easily, and there were her children looking at each other from either side. She'd tell me their names, though I knew them by heart, and then I'd close the locket with a satisfying snip, and lean against her chest, which was a pillow of soft bosom, and she'd pat me. Fred had tattoos from when he was a sailor, and he let me trace them with my fingertips, the dark-green ink fading and blurring. His glasses were thick and heavy, and he'd let me look through them and squint at the room that would suddenly swim in front of me. We think they were from somewhere near Tyne, but now I wonder if we had that right, and why we didn't think to properly ask and get a real history. You don't think about that when you're a child. You don't see adults as walking, breathing history museums. They exist in the space of a moment with you, and what you look for is the way they listen and teach you. Now I wish I knew all of their story, because the hole in my memory of them makes them feel farther away.

Fred, his lungs full of asbestos, died when I was eleven years old. He would only have been in his early seventies. It was the first funeral I had been to. I sat next to my dad and giggled because I couldn't process the grief I felt all around me. I remembered when we'd celebrated Massey and Fred's fiftieth wedding anniversary and they let me eat one of the sugar bells that adorned the top of the cake. I thought about Fred's tanned forearms and tattoos. I looked at Massey and she was crying. I had never seen her cry. At the reception afterwards the room was very quiet, and the sound the cups and saucers made seemed like the only noise in the world.

Sometimes now I text my mother to ask about her memories of Massey and Fred. She tells me little things I have forgotten, and reminds me of Fred's hands, and we remember their roughness and deep grooves. I feel myself back in their house in an instant, and hear his gentle voice. His imprint is still with us, this adopted grandad, and I feel his loss as keenly as if he had just been taken, feel the sadness in the words from my mother.

Massey survived Fred by seven years. When we went to see her, she would peep her head through the net curtain in the kitchen at the sound of our car, and I always noticed this because it used to be the two of them there, framed in welcome. The spaces in the house held Fred's absence, too. His chair still smelt like him, and when I opened the drawer of the bureau to retrieve the dominoes it felt as if he was at my shoulder. Massey longed to be with him, and she told me how much she missed him. By now I was a teenager, and much of what I learned about longing I learned from Massey. Though we tried to occupy her, I saw her sadness, and I could feel her spirit drift away, looking for him in the holes he'd left in the house.

Massey ended up in hospital with a broken hip, and

caught pneumonia. We went to visit her at Middlemore, in the rooms that smelt of cleaning fluid and used tissues. I hated saying goodbye, and after the others had left the room I would run back to see her, drawing the curtain back until I could see her face. The last time I did that we just gazed at each other in silence, and I absorbed her goodbye as clearly as if she had spoken it out loud. I felt her memorise my face, and I did the same with hers: the way the oxygen mask pressed into the slack skin of her cheeks, her eyes filmy and searching, her soft hair close to her head. Her mouth moved as if to make a smile, but it was too much effort. I smiled for both of us and told her how much I loved her. By the time we were home, she was gone.

Sometimes I still dream about that room, and the curtain, and her eyes. For many years the memory made me cry, but now when it comes back to me I think about how she set me on my path in the months before she died. By then I was at drama school, out in the world and finding my place. She told me several times that I was the strong one, and it was my job to look after everyone in the family and to keep us all together. I wonder now if she knew she would leave us soon and wanted to get us ready. She'd tell me out of the blue, perhaps when we were walking from the car to the house, or while we were sitting at the table after dinner, bowls being put out for dessert. I didn't understand what she meant at the time, but later I saw how I became the fighter for my family. I took her words seriously, and wore them with responsibility.

After her funeral, where we kids did the best job we could with a eulogy, I fought with my family. We came back to the house Mum and Dad were renting while their new house was being built, and my grief stretched too wide for the room. I was wild with anger that Massey was gone, so I started a fight and left, racing in my car to Dad's office where I lived out the back in a small bedsit. I drew my blankets around me and cried until I fell asleep. In the night I woke and felt the familiar pressure down the end of the bed, in the corner where Massey would sit to read me stories, or later, when I was grown, to say goodnight to me. In the darkness I could just make out the shape of her body there, solid and steady. I lay in the cocoon of my sheets and talked to her until I fell asleep again. When I woke up in the morning she had gone, but her reminder to be strong had come back to me, and I got in my car and went back to see my family.

After Massey died, I tucked a photo of her and Fred into my wallet. It had been taken on my sixth birthday, which I remember because I had a new striped jumpsuit to wear. We are on the concrete path that leads to our front door, and Fred is holding me, hoisted up on his hip, and my arm is around his shoulder. Massey has her arm across my stomach, and we all smile for the camera. These are my grandparents, and here is the great love we shared, shining out of the photograph. I carried that photo with me everywhere for over a decade, until I found a frame for it and hung it on the wall above my bed. I still have some of the birthday cards they gave me, too, the writing growing more spidery by the year, but the best wishes and the love the same.

Love from Massey and Fred.

Love from Massey.

It was usually a Sunday that we would go to visit Dad's mum. On any given weekend Mum would have a bag of clothes she'd bought for Nana: some new underwear that seemed impossibly large for such a little lady, another blouse, or a soft cardigan. Sometimes we took chocolates for her, or baking, and we carried these offerings like devotionals, stepping with care through the brown-tinted sliding doors at the rest-home entrance. My sister and I would glance at one another when the familiar scent reached our nostrils: old clothes pressed into cupboards to muster, some kind of soup always on the go in the kitchen, the smell of baby powder that seemed incongruous around such old people, the close air exhaled from ancient lungs again and again.

Most days we found Nana in the lounge area, where residents were gathered in their chairs and wheelchairs in little clumps around the room. Sometimes Nana was alone, and though it always worried me, I knew she didn't notice absence anymore. We said hello and I watched my dad's face as he greeted her, searching her expression for signs she recognised him. Most of the time she didn't, but she turned her head to look at each of us in turn, remembering at least how introductions go. I felt Dad's heaviness on these days. I was tuned into his sadness as if it were a radio station, and I would lean into him, lending him the support of my limbs, though I was only small.

Mum would go to deliver the clothes, and to have a word with the nurses, to see how Nana had been and to ask what had happened to all her other knickers. She had her name written in marker on the insides of them, but it seemed that all the underwear become communal after the first wash. I saw my parents exchange glances of exasperation but also of guilt. They had not wanted to put her in a home. But Nana needed constant assistance; she would try to get away in the night, and in the day, too, if she was not watched. She was disoriented, but always trying to find her way back somewhere. Dad thought she was trying to get home to the little house in Howick that her sons built for her.

On sunny days we would wrap a blanket around her legs and take her for a walk around the grounds and up the street a way so she could feel the breeze and the sunlight. We took turns to push the wheelchair, and Nana would settle into the rhythm of the rolling and begin to nod her head. She nodded very slowly, her chin all the way down to her chest, before she lifted her head and began the slow journey to plant her gaze on the sky. She did this without stopping, while my parents kept up a stream of chatter, always trying to reach her, to prompt her memory with names and stories. Her memory was somewhere we couldn't reach. We'd take her back to the home, and while my parents organised payments and wrote new lists of items she needed, we'd go wandering around the room.

My sister and I were magnets for old people, and we stopped to say hello and hold the hands of the residents who reached out to us. Some of them mistook us for their relatives, and we froze in embarrassment but smiled and tried not to upset them. There was one old man who never had a visitor on Sundays, and who I feared never had a visitor at all. If I couldn't find him in the lounge I'd walk the wide avenues of corridors looking for him and his big smile full of false teeth. I didn't know his name. The days I didn't see him I would wonder if he had died. I learned about death in this care home, where the paper name tags slipped into the silver holders on the doors changed regularly, and the faces of Nana's neighbours were different almost every week.

After we'd said our goodbyes, I'd turn to look back at her, and see she had a faint smile on her face and was looking at her hands. On the car ride home, Dad told us stories of how ferocious she was as a younger woman, how she disciplined them and the funny things she would say. There was always admiration in his voice for how she managed to raise six boys on her own. Dad was the youngest, so got to spend the most one-on-one time with his mother after his brothers left home. It pained him he couldn't do more for her, but not as much as it pained him when she didn't recognise him.

On some of those Sundays, Massey and Fred came round for a fish and chip dinner. Massey showed me how to drizzle malt vinegar over my portion, and I sat beside her and watched the way she ate hot chips with gusto, so very alive.

The room was full of the chatter you'd hope for when three generations gather—about stories being read, and how school was going, and how it had been since we were last together. There was laughter, and comfort in the takeaway ritual, but I always thought about what Nana was eating a few suburbs away. We were never there for meal times and I wondered if she ate alone, or someone helped her the way we helped my little brother, making sure he chewed and swallowed and didn't rush.

After one of those dinners I asked if we could take fish and chips to Nana the next time we went to see her. Dad said we could, and he held my hand tight under the table.

The first serious boyfriend I had was in possession of a very wonderful grandfather, and at twenty I gravitated toward him like a moth to a lamp. Abuelo was in his mid seventies, and he lived in a cottage a few streets over from my boyfriend's parents in Waipukurau. He also had big thick glasses, which I think I assumed was prerequisite for grandads, and he wore a peaked tweed cap. He sat in the sun on his front porch, walking stick knocked against his leg, and when he'd see us come up the path he'd smile in a wry way and then try to find something he could feed us. When we visited, we drank Fanta, which he poured with much ceremony, exclaiming 'Fanta Fanta Fanta!' in his soft Chilean accent. He taught me how to cook alcachofas—artichokes—boiling them in salted water until the leaves were tender. We set the artichokes on a plate and pulled the wet leaves away from the stem, dipping them in oil and vinegar, running our teeth along the fleshy part, separating it from the fibrous leaf. He also taught me how to cook rice, sautéeing a little garlic in some butter before adding the grains of rice to coat them, then adding the water, the result fluffy and rich. When my boyfriend and I broke up, I probably grieved more for losing Abuelo than I did for him.

—

At forty-one I inherit a set of grandparents following my marriage. In their sitting room I kneel on the floor and tuck blankets around their thin legs, and rearrange pillows, and offer cups of tea and accompanied visits to the bathroom. My new grandfather, Bapa, is pretty deaf, and he leans closer to hear me, smiling as I try to show in gestures what I want to say. When he speaks it is only to say hello, or thank you, and his voice sounds like the scratch of autumn leaves blown along the road. I sit on the floor beside the checkerboard and watch his long, thin fingers knock away Arun's counters as he slides his own into their spaces, growing a pile of discards beside him, winning, but only just. In some games he is certain that he is playing the other colour counters, and will not be told, and then some way through he remembers and plays his side again. He gazes at the board as if it holds his whole life, though all it holds is time passing.

Ways to fill in the hours when you are one hundred and three—that is what none of us can give him. He plays Solitaire on an iPad while my new grandmother, Mai, dozes in her swing seat, her sari wrapping her legs and waterfalling over her shoulder in soft blue folds. She sleeps with her head back, as if she is craning her neck at heaven. When she falls, as she does more often now that tumours press on her brain, she asks us why God hasn't taken her yet. She asks in Gujarati, and Arun translates for me, and we hold her hands and try to make jokes. When she fell badly before we were married, we told her God hadn't taken her because he wanted her to come to our wedding. She laughed, and for a moment forgot the bandages wrapping her forehead, where her skin is as thin as vellum.

Her eyes are bright like a blackbird's, and they follow me around the living room while I wet dust and vacuum. I go to clean their little flat, which is attached to the main family home, because the country is in lockdown for Covid-19 and the cleaners can't come. We are part of an extended bubble who come to care for them, to take the pressure off Arun's mother and sister who do the lion's share of the work. I clean the basins and toilets, wipe down the kitchen bench and table, and hang the washing out while they slip in and out of sleep. For two people so old they are stubborn about their independence, and I have to be quick to catch them when they are on the move to the bathroom, in case they fall. The hospital is no place for centenarians.

On the news and on social media arguments surface about letting the elderly be the casualty of this pandemic, because they are aging out of the world anyway and it is better for them to die than young people. My mother, at seventy-two, is now classed in this bracket, too, and I feel horror when I see the bloodless way lives are discussed as if they are disposable. Arun's grandparents helped to raise him. They lived in his family home for his entire life, and cared for him, and taught him things that have no monetary value but yield dividends in wisdom and guardianship. My mother has five grandchildren who dote on her, who sob over Skype during lockdown because they miss her so badly. When they are reunited they refuse to leave her, clinging like loving barnacles. I watch the way the world splits in two, one side cherishing the lives of our most vulnerable, and the other eager to dispense with them, and I am sick.

The oldest among us hold the memories of times the rest of us can only read about. They are witnesses to history; their cells contain years no one else can reach. In their skin, my new grandparents hold journeys by ship from

Gujarat to Auckland, many months at sea between world wars. Theirs is an immigrant story and a love story, six children and a new life in New Zealand. I cannot imagine trivialising their lives because it's time they shuffled off anyway. I can't imagine trivialising anyone's life, yet I see it every day on the news, in bulletins from around the world where leaders and so-called pundits expound on the figures of infected and dead in their countries. In Sweden, two-thirds of the several thousand dead are the elderly. In New Zealand it is the rest homes hit the hardest as the death toll, modest as it is, slowly climbs. Locked in for their own safety, the elderly are also locked in to a virus that sweeps through as if they were made of nothing more substantial than air. Each time another death is linked to one of the rest-home clusters I feel weight press my heart to a wet, dull thudding. I imagine the gripping fear and loneliness. The world goes on, apparently, and we commit experience to dust and let them die alone.

I make cups of tea, and take extra care to clean the bathroom mirror.

On Friday afternoons I go round just to spend time and to keep an eye on them. I am clumsy with my basic Gujarati, but manage to say hello and ask how they are. My mother-in-law teaches me how to make the traditional chai tea they like to drink, and I spoon the spice mix and black tea in small measures into a saucepan with water, sugar and milk. It blooms in brown fragrant bubbles, and the scent presses close, and that's how I know it's ready.

In the later part of the day they watch television, which is mostly gameshows, and I sit with them and watch the sun make shapes on the carpet through the sari that is drying on the line outside the lounge. Mai watches an advertisement for an air fryer, and shakes her head, gesturing to me how ridiculous it is. She likes to fry food in oil and thinks the dry fryer is an outrage. This much I understand. I have no language, but some days I feel we know each other in the smiles, hand patting, and silly gestures I make to express myself. They indulge me, I know. They are tired, and sleep often, but whenever I come, they make the effort to be there for a moment and to smile at me before they rest again.

Mai and Bapa have been married for eighty-five years, one of the longest marriages in the world today. They came to our wedding, these ancient lovers, and it felt like a blessing for a long life. Amidst the congratulations cards from our families we found one from them, Bapa's scrawl wishing us all the best, and telling us how proud he was, how we have made him happy. On a slip of paper inside the card was a message from Mai. I tucked it away for a day when it could be translated in her company, and remembered how she told Arun he ought to marry me the first time I met her.

Bapa turns one hundred and four, and we eat fish and chips, gathering in the sitting room, passing him and Mai glasses of lemonade, everyone chatting, speaking in loud voices so that he can understand. Mai shows me a photograph of her as a young woman surrounded by her siblings. She tells me their names, her expression changing as she points out which ones have died. I wish I could ask her questions about her life. I ask Arun, and he tells me in fits and starts about their life in India, where Bapa was a fighter in Gandhi's freedom army. It's hard to imagine him as a young rebel, but in the fading photos on the wall he is handsome, and his eyes are steady and intelligent.

After another spell in hospital and the realisation that Mai needs twenty-four-hour hospital care, the process begins to try to find a care home for her and Bapa too. Everyone agrees it's remarkable they have managed to stay at home all this time, but the sadness as the family gathers to talk through options is palpable. I feel the tears gather, as if the room is weeping. Next door Bapa sleeps, with a blanket around his legs, alone for the longest time anyone can remember, while Mai recovers in hospital and plans are made for the next part of their story.

Most of the rest homes are full, and the Covid-19 safety measures are so necessarily strict that, in the end, the best choice is to bring in full-time carers and keep Mai and Bapa in their own home where family can be with them. One of the carers speaks Gujarati, and it feels like the gift everyone needed after so much difficulty. Mai and Bapa's beds now crowd the sitting room, and the second storey of the house is committed to the memory of a time when stairs were still assailable. The room is warm on the first day I visit; I chat to a carer and make chai tea. I put pikelets on a plate, smoothing them with butter, and try to encourage Mai to eat. She resists. She is tired but pats my hand as she always has. Bapa sleeps. Later, on the family group chat, messages are exchanged about meals being cooked for them: soupy fish, papadi saak, moong. I read the words passed back and forth across the afternoon, the expressions of worry and care and love, and see the way nurture is exchanged across generations.

When Arun's mother buys new thermal singlets for Bapa and a cardigan for Mai, I see Mum bringing clothes to Nana in the home. Bapa smiles at me from his chair, worn hands grasping his walking stick, and I feel the memory of Fred stir in another sitting room decades ago. I rearrange the blanket across Mai's knees, tucking it under her feet, and remember how Massey always tucked me in before she said goodnight. In the warm sitting room the centenarians sleep and I keep watch for them, and I keep watch over the memories of my own grandparents, and feel how their love lives inside me still, bright in my bones, and shining.

Hide and Speak

At some point you make a decision to vanish. You go out into the landscape of story and leave yourself behind. You do it consciously, slipping out of the clothes of your skin and into the forms of others. You let them talk to you. They choose your music, dictate the way you move and what you eat. You take a stranger's physiology and you swallow it, let the shape of a new person enter your cells by osmosis, spreading out from your insides, blanketing familiar spaces with their uncommon rhythm and strange-smelling breath. Out in that landscape, in these new poses, you make fresh meaning of the ordinariness of being human, and you find stillness.

It is uncomplicated to be someone else. In a stranger's skin you can stretch into places your own being has barricaded; you try out these new liberties and admire the way they look on you. You seem carefree. You can run amok if you want to, and you can't get into trouble, except in the story. You flip the switch only in your dreams, when you return to yourself and your deep unconscious, and your ordinary life sends you messages about jobs that need doing round the house or phone calls you're yet to make. In this way you live with duality: in possession of two lives at any given time, and always with somewhere to run to, you dip between realities like a bee dips between flower heads. In story you are in pollen, and in your lived existence you look for the scatters of golden yellow, for a trail to lead you away.

When I was very young I stopped talking—just stopped altogether and hid between my mother's legs when family came to visit. Several weeks went by and I never said a word. I remember my mother shaking me out of her skirts like an insect who had got caught there. I remember the blue sea at the hem, and pressing my face to the sun umbrellas and beach balls scattered over it, this summer skirt I wouldn't part with. Picking up the murmur of adult voices from behind my fabric barricade, I thought everyone was annoyed at me, but now I wonder if my deep shyness had always been evident, and this extension, this flare during a visit from our Californian cousins, was just something they observed as they would a cat doing something new:

with curiosity. After the cousins went back to America, the shyness wore off, and nobody said much about it at all. It came back to me at school, at sports events especially, and it came to me when we had visitors at home, when Dad brought people he'd met overseas to dinner. I used to lie in bed listening for the farewells at the front door, waiting for the outside light to turn off—the sign the visitors had gone. The pitch into darkness was a relief, and the sounds of my parents tidying up in the kitchen a comfort.

I learned much later, listening to the radio in my car, that those spells are called selective mutism and are brought on by anxiety. They are more common in children. When I suffered those patches of quietness, the only way to draw me out was through story. Every evening we sat down with books. Dad occupied the middle of the couch, and we climbed up around him, settling into shapes of eagerness. He would read every story character with a voice of its own, with specific tics and quirks, sound effects and cadences. We listened intently for the choices he would make each time. We got to know the rhythms of story, the way the momentum would gather and build to a conclusion, and we would wait, squirming, for the exciting moments we knew were coming, shouting the words alongside him.

He handed characters to us. He handed me Dinglemouse in *Badjelly the Witch*, and it was the first character I ever played, taking it seriously, checking his reaction as I read the words. I climbed into the body of that mouse and I left my own in a rumpled heap on the floor.

On that expedition I could feel the wind in my fur, and see the faces of the other characters moving with expression. I felt euphoria as the words came from me and filled the world, animating the story all around me. Afterwards, when the stories were finished, I'd lay them in piles next to my bed, and dangle my arm down beneath the duvet so that my fingertips brushed the covers in my sleep.

I have kept every one of my books from childhood. Many of them have lost their covers; the sellotape that holds them together has become brown and brittle. The chapter books have felt-tip pen squiggles in the margins, and the dog-eared edges have worn away from sharp corners to round tabs. The picturebook jackets have faded in the sun, but the illustrations inside still bloom in lustrous colour. If I open a book and place my hand on an illustration, I can go back in time and remember one of the days when I read it. I feel it in my skin and in my muscles, and my body hunches to take the shapes of my then-small form in space.

There is a book called *Sir Squirrel*, about some woodland creatures, and I only have to touch it to be back in our little study, in our old house before it was renovated, wrapped into a snail shape on the green corded couch, clutching a Milo and turning the pages. The room was a mess, and my mother was cross. Felt-tip pen marks had been found on the wallpaper behind the couch. Everyone was in trouble. The day I read *Sir Squirrel* there, I spilt a big drop of Milo on the page where all the animals dress up for the ball. If I run my fingers over the splash I can recall Mum's tight-mouthed annoyance and her silence in the kitchen, and how I hauled my pink flowergirl dress out, and walked down the hallway to meet Sir Squirrel. I saw the white staircase and stepped up it. I went to the ball.

My mother enrolled me in drama classes when I was five, wondering if it might draw me out of the snug shell of my shyness. In the huge hall with wooden floors, I inspected the corners of the room for mysteries, and came forward reluctantly when it was my turn. Our teacher, Gair, was a tiny woman capable of terrific magic and strictness. She had her hair short in a pixie cut, and she wore pants, only ever pants, so she could move around the room quickly, and tuck her legs up beneath her when she went outside to smoke. It was from her I learned how to speak and be heard, to finish the ends of my words with sharp clarity. All the games we played were imagination games. I lost myself in those palaces and pigsties we built. In character I found the way to slip my skin, and become someone else, someone brave and bold. It was a kind of bewitchment. In the same way that children think that if their eyes are shut nobody can see them, I thought pretending to be someone else meant I disappeared from view.

I don't know that I was particularly good at it, but I was devoted to acting. I was as close to the stories as I could be, swallowed up inside them, hidden, yet speaking their words from the inside. I never revealed to anyone this new way to disappear, but I fostered it. Now when I picked up books I tried to imagine how it would be, in the skin of every character I read. Age seven I was allowed to be in a proper play. The place where I took drama lessons had a small theatre attached to it. It was an enchanted space to us kids. The floors were dusty planks of kauri, and the apron of the stage was the demarcation line where the sets were built back into the dark recess of space. The audience sat in gently raised seating, up up up toward the technician's box, where you could see someone peering through the little glass window, waiting for their cues to dim the lights and swell the music. We didn't have a curtain, but we had 'flats', oblong stands covered in black fabric, used in the wings to hide the actors as we came and went from the stage.

It was behind these we crowded, peering through the tiny tears in the fabric to see the audience. My palms would be rinsed in sweat, and I'd wipe them on my costume. My heart would swell and pound so loudly I thought I would get told off, or explode. I couldn't see how I could make my body go out there. But Gair would be pacing backstage, stalking us, making us focus, her expression ferocious. The first foot I placed into the flood of lights made me forget myself and forget to be afraid. The lights were dazzling, the ambush of lumens seared my eyes and poured into my body, illuminating my insides where the character was hiding. I found someone, and she was all of me and no part of me at once.

In that first play I was a guard in a court, and a street seller carrying a basket and peddling primroses. We were in London at the time of the plague. I had children at home and a sick husband. We needed the money from the flowers to buy medicine for his chest. It mattered to sell every last bundle. Imaginary lives depended on it. Cobblestones had been painted on the floor to show what the streets were like back then. I stepped lightly, imagining the sound of my boots on the cold stone. I had just a few words to say—'Primroses! Two bundles a penny! Primroses!' It was magic.

I look back at photos and I'm not fooling anyone. My sparse, cowlicked fringe sticks out through the piece of fabric tied to look like a headscarf. The flowers in the basket are obviously fake. I am seven years old, pretending to be an adult. It must have been a painful show to watch. All my family came, and filled a row. At half-time they had gingernuts and instant coffee or tea or cordial in the lobby. That must have been the best bit about it. They came every time, though, as I progressed through many tiny roles—as a non-speaking mermaid in *Peter Pan*, or a moth in a play about insects. I was always very excited to play several roles and not have many lines.

Around this time, I was under the spell of *The Lion, The Witch and the Wardrobe*. I had a purple hardback copy that I carted around with me everywhere. It seemed the perfect witchcraft—to climb into a wardrobe and emerge in another country altogether, feeling the soft fur of coats give way to the rough bark of trees. C. S. Lewis's professor tells Peter and Susan that 'nothing is more probable' than the idea that there are other worlds just around the corner. I found it to be true, and every time I pulled on a costume it became my portal. The wardrobe was real, but it was clothing I climbed into, not a cupboard, to find myself in new terrain.

Coming down from the highs of imaginary worlds became increasingly difficult as I got older. I struggled so much in my teenage form. My very skin felt unbearable. But every time we did a theatre show I could escape. It was intoxicating. Days when we did a matinee as well as an evening performance were heaven. They meant hours and hours as someone else, and in the breaks between performances, still covered in crude make-up and slicked with hair gel, we'd all wander up to the dairy and buy pies and bags of chips, and I'd feel my character tugging at me, nudging me with their shoulder, daring me to be them out in the world, not to let them go.

I grew bolder, allowing their voice to be mine in public spaces, walking back to the theatre in their stride, crossing roads, encountering stares from strangers with their self-possession. There's a trope we often see in cinema when the story concerns theatre actors: they're bright with stage make-up, and calling loudly to each other in dressing rooms, posturing, smoking and behaving provocatively. When I see those portrayals it reminds me of walking down the road in half-character, with a kind of swagger and invincibility because the story still has you. You are untouchable. I think it's a state all actors inhabit, and that's why it turns up again and again in representations on screen.

It was a tired kind of heaven I experienced, coming back to myself in the evenings, standing on the street waiting for the lights of Mum's car to come up the hill. Crashing into sleep with tide lines of make-up at the edges of my hair and the oily scent of Pond's cream in my nose. I felt the boundaries of another universe at my elbows, and in my dreams I heard the words and felt them tip my consciousness. I dreamt of being trapped in myself, marooned in my own body with no way to escape, and woke gasping, worried I would be locked into my own form forever.

When Dad was dying he asked for our old Famous Five books. Some afternoons I'd find him on the couch, thumbing through those stories, finding comfort in regression toward a simpler time. He'd ask me if I remembered this particular book, and together we'd pass the parts of the story back and forth between us. He wasn't eating much, but we'd talk about the food in the books: the ginger beer and the sandwiches, the fruit cake and the hardboiled eggs. He was halfway through *Five Run Away Together* when he died, a scrap of paper marking his place. I put it back on the bookshelf, where the sum of the stories is the balance of my entire childhood as well as his. They are a living memory into which we pass, and then pass over. The story of my dad and the books becomes a narrative of its own, kept company in the volumes that crowd the bookcases in my house. I go looking for him in those stories and I find his reassurance in their bucolic adventures and their innocence. He's there in the rowboats and the islands. He's in the castle ruins and the cottages. He is the sixth member of the expedition, and I am the seventh, trailing after him.

—

We don't think about the way that story conceals us. Often we talk about what story reveals—about ourselves, about the nature of the world. But I found story to be the abyss into which I could crawl, fill myself up with words and ideas, and paper over myself with pages. I became the story. It is a common misconception that actors like to show off, be seen, and to maintain visibility at all times. The best actors I know are quiet, often-worried people. I sense in some actors I meet that it is painful to exist in this present moment. That they are out of time with the whole world, and anxious to be back in a bridging universe that links real life to the imaginary, where they belong. I am like that, often.

The best characters are the ones farthest away from

yourself. It is a stretch to reach them; their ideas, their moral compass, their behaviour is so different from your own. When you make acquaintance with them, you must be cautious and feel out the edges of their ambitions, observe without judgement the things they covet, and then do your best to get those things for them. You learn to love their recklessness. You revel in the way they are fearless in taking on anyone. You appreciate their deadly wit, and let the words they speak wound people. You take their side, because in the end they have no one else—they only have you to breathe life into them. You take their side because you'd choose them over yourself any day.

I don't prescribe to any kind of method, but I let each character inform the shady parts of my life. They exist in my shadow on days when I am off set, and I feel them judge me. On a whim I take up activities I think they would approve of. When playing a cat–human hybrid with excellent martial-arts skills, I take classes at the gym where I can move my body to a fight prescription, punching bags, leaping around, kicking the air. I am not as coordinated as I am on set, where I have a fight choreographer and a stunt crew putting me through my paces, but I get fitter and faster, and leaner, and I know my character is pleased with me, because I sweat less under my heavy wig and make-up, and the fighting gets easier each week.

I watch Bruce Lee films, and then Jet Li films. I watch as many action films as I can, and absorb a kind of physicality I have never met before; my body is agile and practical, I am as compact as a cat and I waste no energy. When, after a year in her skin, I let her go, she wanders off in the way you'd expect from a cat, without a backwards glance. In the weeks afterwards my body settles down, and the muscles that have hardened in tight ropes begin to soften. I pour my attention into the kitten I bought at the start of the project, inhaling the scent of his fur, watching him move with delicate precision.

I play a Norse goddess with a chip on her shoulder and I become acquainted with the lush in myself. I buy expensive wine that I know nothing about. I buy new figure-hugging clothes because she is secure in her form and revels in her sexuality. I am not promiscuous but I think about what it would be like if I were. I think about ignoring all the social rules, being as bold as she is, and as certain with men. Toward the end of the first season, I allow myself a mild promiscuity and try out my learned sexual confidence at parties, where I behave in ways I never usually would. I go home for Sunday lunch at my parents' house feeling aggrieved. Nice girls from Howick don't get up to these things—but, under her guidance, I do, and for a brief time I feel untouchable. I feel it is for me Sylvia Plath wrote:

And I eat men like air.

And then she is gone. After three seasons in her skin—her volatile, difficult, caustic and wildly free skin—she leaves me. I shuffle back into tracksuit pants, and tie my hair up into messy knots again. I spend more time in my spectacles and less time in make-up. I drink beer and volunteer at a bird sanctuary.

When the character is closer to you, there is difficulty. Their worries almost match your own, and they can sneak in when you're not looking. Their worry makes you wonder if you should also be worried—they are, after all, your own age. They are concerned about having children before it is too late. They are worried they are unlovable. They fear they will never have a relationship that lasts. They are anxious that they will be alone and the pain of it will consume them. They fill up their life in being busy for other people—running a restaurant, volunteering for the ambulance, elected to town councils. They fill their life to mask how alone they are.

I tried to match that. I tried out being sociable, really engaged with life and people. I attended lectures and festivals and dinners and fun runs. I started a book club, just like she did. I filled up my hours, even as I came home each evening to my parents' house, where I lived in those months on the job. When my dad got sick I tried to think about how she would process it. I got busier, doing everything I could for him, involving myself in every decision. I became the bulldog for my family, pushing for answers with a warm but determined smile. It was exhausting but I filled up the hours, and the only time I was alone was when I put my head down at night to sleep. When she left me, I felt the loss. I didn't know what to do with myself. She fell away in pieces until I was myself again, and not busy enough to keep tamping my emotions down. I came back to myself and I fell apart.

There are things that are required of you from time to time. You are asked to attend awards, in gowns, on carpets, to smile and to answer questions, to promote and enhance. People are there to help you look your best; you spend hours in the chair being dabbed at with brushes and blown out under heat, before squeezing into a dress that suits many other people more than it suits you. You hope you'll be photographed so you can show strangers on social media and thank the designer who lent you the dress. Your value becomes less about the work and more about the commodity you have become: you are a walking advertisement dressed up in jewels. It seems a corruption to be employed to hide in someone else's skin, and then to have to come out naked in your own form. Completely vulnerable and without the armour of character, you trot out like a prized horse, ribbons fluttering. It is the opposite of everything you like.

I used to watch awards shows when I was young. I'd watch the women saunter and smoulder in gowns so spun with colour and endless metres of fabric they looked like confection out there on the carpet. The male actors grinned, hands in the pockets of their much easier suits. I understood it was part of the work. I was excited about the dresses and the glamour, but when it was my turn to prance around at much less opulent awards shows, I froze. That old mutism came back, and I'd hug the sideline as much as I could, wanting so much to enjoy it but feeling unbearably nude. The trick was to get several drinks down you, glide out there like you were some kind of swan on a canal, cruising along the length of carpet, getting through it with a wide smile and shoulders at pleasing angles.

Nobody ever knew my name, and I felt embarrassed when I had to spell it, laboriously sounding out the letters. I briefly wondered if anyone would notice if I gave them a false one. Once you'd got inside, you could have another drink and dissolve into the crowds of much more famous people, effectively vanishing as part of the decorative set. You could sit at tables with your castmates and observe the people who had starved themselves into shape for this day get drunk on small glasses of wine. I would watch the awards and watch the clock, wishing it were an ordinary weeknight and I could go home to bed, setting my alarm early for filming.

I always found a way to get out as swiftly as possible, to get to the hotel room and eat burgers in my pyjamas, my make-up still on but my hair undone, the dress, unbothered, hung in the wardrobe, the shoes, unwearable, back in the box. I ducked out of awards nights often when

I lived in Sydney, catching cabs home with other New Zealand actors, hauling on track pants and sitting at the kitchen counter to eat slice after slice of Marmite on toast. We'd drink vodka neat from tumblers and talk about other things—things that had nothing to do with acting at all. In the mornings, dutiful, I'd look for a photo and put it online, thank everyone involved, and then hide for weeks.

At times I have got through by pretending to be someone else. It was not so much that I played a character, but that I tried to channel someone else's confidence. I went through an embarrassing stage of trying to invoke Anaïs Nin when I went to events—I thought she was someone who wouldn't give a damn about any of it, and hoped her insouciance would rub off on me. It didn't. I once hid in a bathroom at a party held by my agent. I hid there for thirty-five minutes. I cut my fringe with manicure scissors in the small mirror blooming with green rot at the edges. I sorted through the receipts in my wallet. I skulked out when I knew I couldn't hold off any longer. Any time I have to go somewhere and I'm feeling nervous, invariably someone will say, 'But you're an actor, you must be used to this!' I can't account for the magic of the vanishing. It is a neat trick that's thrown down: a swift sleight of hand and I'm gone.

When we were planning our wedding, I wanted to elope and to say our vows somewhere in another city, anonymous in an office. I realised we wouldn't be able to do that as soon as my future mother-in-law got teary when we joked about it. We chose to have a tiny family wedding, mostly because we were afraid we would lose one or both of Arun's grandparents if we had a long engagement. I didn't want to say my vows in front of lots of people anyway. I didn't want everybody looking at me. At that moment I couldn't pretend to be anyone else; I had to hold my centre and exchange vows as myself. I just find it easier to do important, public-facing things as someone else. I've played characters who've had to talk to a room full of people and it's been no trouble at all because I am not myself. I've delivered long monologues on stage and not felt any discomfort, only abandon in the flow of words and ideas. I've worn provocative clothes and said outrageous things on camera and never blinked an eye. In my own skin, though, I am shy.

It took me thirty-two years to start writing, but when I did it I felt a blow of recognition across my body. The force of realisation was so strong it reconfigured my cells and made my synapses do dance routines in my brain. I had taken six months away from acting; I was bone-weary and I wanted to try something new. I sat in a classroom with about twenty other students, and our writing teacher asked us to imagine a mantelpiece and then put objects on it—whatever came into our heads. Then we focused on one of the objects, and its history became part of the first short story we wrote. I heard a voice start talking in my head, start telling me things about this object, and I listened and I wrote them down. I heard him clear as a bell. I listened for the cadence of his speech in the same way I listen for it in the characters I inhabit. I let him reveal himself to me. He told me his story and I was in his world with him, side by side, looking at the things he wanted to show me. I set my brain on fire with that one small act, and I walked through it burning with words and the understanding that I had found another way to be in the story.

I find comfort in the way words come together to form rhythms and arcs. The way they commune to make a story is a witchcraft I have always witnessed but now am part of. Words are good company. I hide in them, crouching behind the letters that spill out from under my fingertips. I do not write fiction. I save the imaginary worlds for when I work as an actor. The writing class gave me a glimpse of how to tell a story, whether mine or someone else's. I grow greedy for the stories of people I meet. I ask too many questions at dinner tables. I store the things I glean from strangers and examine them at home, turning them over to see the shape they take. Some days I walk down the street and allow myself to imagine every passerby as a bundle of fluttering pages. At the traffic lights I wait for the pedestrian crossing to turn green, and I watch all the pages of story crossing with me, ruffling in the breeze, stepping out with their paper dogs on leads. There they go up the street, the stories of all those lives. I want to snatch them and hold them to me. I want to write them all down before they are lost.

When we are gone, the stories about us replace the imprint of our bodies in time and space. The whole of the world is a gigantic, invisible library of books about the whole of the world. I write the stories of myself, and disappear into my skin in times and places that exist now only in memory. I live again in my body as a young, shy child, and I feel the silence of my throat and the world clamouring around me. The words on the page are an invitation that I accept each time I write them. I dip between the flower heads with the bees, and come out pollen-cloaked and golden. I go to the ball.

Mother/ Earth

We were taught to watch out for the living. We pored over little lives the way you'd pore over the words of a book—words that grew stems and legs, antennae and stamens. I thought *flora* and *fauna* were words my mother had invented especially for the life in our garden. My mother, down in the dirt on her knees, gloved fingers turning bulbs into the soil or tearing out weeds. I could crouch beside her, and she'd show me the roots of the invaders as she dislodged them, the long pale tentacles that reached towards an underground dream we could not be part of. My mother, who I was sure was part tree, because before I was born her shins had been pierced by ponga, which had to be cut out by a doctor, while the flesh of her legs puffed pink and shiny, her body seeming to try to cover over the intrusion points and swallow them up, talking the tree into her body, asking the trunks to run through her bones with the calcium.

I used to look for the scars on her legs, but her tan skin was freckled and I could never be sure where the ponga had tried to get into her. I asked Dad to tell me the story of how they split the logs and how the pieces lodged in her skin, and he'd tell me how tough my mother was. She would tell me how she never touched a ponga again after that. At the garden centre I used to run my fingers across the trimmed ponga trunks, testing the sharp spines against the pads of my fingers. I'd snap off a spine and lay it along my shin, imagining it shooting up my veins, making its way towards my heart like an arrow.

My mother, with legs she said were bandy, coming into the laundry with dirt caking her feet and sweat on her neck. My mother sowing seeds in cotton wool on the window sill, lifting us up to monitor the daily progress of the cress and mustard, her hand over ours on the scissors when it came time to cut them for sandwiches. My mother handing out jars for us to go down the creek and hunt for tadpoles, calling them taddies, inspecting the jars and hauling out an old glass fish tank from under the house, sending us back to the creek for a bucket of water so the tadpoles could swim in a smaller version of where they'd come from. We watched out for the living because she told us to. We brought things to show her—empty birds' nests, cicada shells, dead bumblebees and weeds we thought were flowers.

'Have a look at this, Mouse' was the most common phrase I heard in childhood, from both my mother and my dad. Summers spent crouching by rock walls, teasing back the pockmarked chunks where they'd come away from the cement, spying on the crickets who sheltered there in the day, their shiny bodies gleaming through the dust. 'Come and look at this,' we'd say, clambering around the garden, finding insect nests to show, plants with unusual leaves, feathers. My mother looking the plants up in a book to tell us their botanical names. Showing us how to dry flowers on the wooden rack in the laundry, where the air always smelt like clothes detergent and Oasis, the florist foam she used for arrangements. The garden was full of flowers, and Mum showed them to us in her book, telling us the stories of how they grew, and how long they would last, what kind of weather they liked and what sort of insects they'd bring.

Some summers, the drying rack became a maternity ward and nursery for monarch butterflies. Attacked by wasps in our garden, and barely managing to survive on dwindling swan plants, the caterpillars were moved indoors to the laundry, where branches of plants we'd found in the wild might satisfy their appetites. They'd fatten, slow down, and make little white hooks to hang off. My mother called us to look. We knew what this meant, and leaned against the bench and watched the way they'd contort their bodies into spiralling shapes, watching for the green split opening along their backs and the shucking of their skins. We cut the branches they hung off, and taped them with care to the top of the drying rack, so they all hung down, dozens of chrysalides safe from the wasps, taking their time to re-form in the primordial slush of their green caves. Some mornings we came down before breakfast and there were handfuls of butterflies drip-drying their wings, the green juice of their cocoons dripping on the laundry bench. We opened the door so they could fly away when they were ready. In time, the laundry smelled more of caterpillars than detergent. My mother didn't mind.

I spent a lot of time in the bush behind our house. It sloped down toward the neighbour's, and curved right in a tangle of trees that ran along the property line to a stream and the back yards of people we didn't know. In the stream were insects that looked as if they were rowing boats across the surface. I built bridges across so I didn't get my feet wet. To get down that far in the bush I had to negotiate with the goat tied up next door who'd make a dash for me, bleating, if he set eyes on me. He was the gatekeeper to a kingdom I wanted to visit, and it became a game to try to distract him by throwing stones across to the opposite side of his grassy bank, drawing his attention away. Other times I'd bribe him with lettuce I'd pinched from the garden.

Down there I sat and listened the way my mother had taught me to, taking in the layers of sound. The bottom notes were the music of insects: bees weaving through the electric rattle of cicadas and the paper flurry of dragonfly wings. Then came the bird sound that was farthest away, in trees I couldn't see: tūī and the soft peeping of pīwakawaka. The top layer was the riroriro, who always seemed to follow me into the bush, their song a cascading trill of notes pouring down the air beside me. I crouched and watched for the bugs and the birds, and pulled at the onion weed to smell its savoury odour. The little flowers no longer tricked me; I knew these were not for taking home to my mother. This was when I would start to lose track of the edges of my body, where it met the ecosystem. This was when, at five, I felt my skin blur and join the air and the forest floor. Through half-closed eyelids I watched as I dissolved into the daylight, my molecules reaching out for the green and the gold, dizzy with the way I was eaten up by the life around me, swallowed whole by the industry of insect cities and plant kingdoms. The architects of oxygen made me giddy. I laid leaves over my eyelids and let them filter the world in green.

When I was six our cat Sophie had kittens under my sister's bed. We found her hiding there with the four slippery wet punctuation marks clinging to her, and were enchanted. I helped to scrub the blood from the carpet after we moved her and the kittens into a warm, towel-lined basket. There was a pink stain forever under my sister's bed—and under mine, where labour had begun but was not concluded. My mother oversaw the health and safety of Sophie and her kittens. If I came quiet upon the room where they rested I'd hear her soft words as she encouraged our mother cat. We kids thought it a miracle, and were in love with the babies. We asked where they came from—Sophie did not have a husband. A few weeks later an illustrated book materialised on the shelf, with pictures of a man and a woman naked, and then a woman naked with a belly, the outline of a baby inside. I didn't know how it related to Sophie, but I studied the pictures and interrogated my mother about who these people were and if we knew them. When the kittens were given away to new homes, our cat spent several months looking for them. She meowed at cupboard doors until we opened them so she could inspect them for her babies. I felt her distress and tried to make it up to her by holding her, and brushing her fur, but she didn't want me, she wanted her children.

I relate more easily to plants and animals than I do to people. It was great luck to be born to a mother who loves living things with a deep blood connection, and who put me near them, in them, on them, at every waking moment. A photo exists of me on the back of a horse, holding on to the tee-shirt of a man who must be in his thirties. I am not quite two years old, and I'm sat up there with a mysterious expression on my face, my legs barely registering on the flanks of the horse I'm so short. I don't remember this time, but I remember every other time I have ridden a horse since.

We'd go out to ride on weekends. Dad drove us to the horse-riding place, and Mum stayed behind at the stables to stroke the noses of the horses who were being rested. I never asked her why she didn't ride, but assumed it was because she doesn't like heights. We came back over the brow of the hill and she was there in the sun. She produced carrots from her jacket pocket and showed me how to hold my hand flat so the horse could snuffle and slime my fingers with eager saliva, nibbling the carrot away from my vulnerable fingers. The teeth looked like piano keys left out in a field. The horse made a whickering noise like he was saying thank you, and I felt his breath on my nose and mouth, and I breathed in too, holding the hour with him closer, not wanting to let go.

Decades later I got a job on a television show in the outback of Australia. My character was not like the other women from the land. She was from the city. But I still had to ride for the storylines. I was put through my paces by a man who said very little, and who, when I asked the horse's name, looked me square in the eye and said, 'It's a horse. It hasn't got one.' I was not allowed to make a point of connection in the way I was used to. There was no time to brush down the horse and clean its hooves and lean against its neck and breathe there, making acquaintance. Instead I was scolded, encouraged, taught to muster and to pull up to marks for the camera. I went through the motions with a heavy, dislocated heart. All around us were sheep and cows and a line of beautiful horses, and I couldn't feel anything at all. I couldn't connect. I was not allowed to.

The earth was hard there. It was deep, and when I stood in bare feet I felt the years of it speaking to my body. I felt its strong motion coursing up my spine. That country had a sturdiness I did not recognise. It strengthened me even as it broke me. The people sounded like the birds, their flat, elongated vowels and nasal calls just like the crows that were everywhere. I squinted in the sunlight that was hard all year round, ran my boots through the dust and watched the treeline where it wavered like water in the heat. I watched the cattle in the field swelter, and I worried. I checked the bores had water. I couldn't help it. At lunchtime the unit tables were piled with meat alongside the salads, and I watched everyone tucking in, while across the paddock the herd moved in the lazy heat. I couldn't relax.

I rode, and I couldn't relax there, either. I nearly herniated a disc in my back from the thumping down on the saddle, pushing my scoliosis curve into a more extreme shape. I could barely walk. The show moved on and I didn't have to ride again. Someone in the crew told me that a horseman we knew drank too much on the weekend and punched his horse in the face. Right in the face like you might punch someone in a pub brawl. It undid me. I felt myself splinter into pieces I was so angry. In breaks on set I went quietly to see the alpacas and the goats and other animals, and apologised to them. I told them I was sorry nobody really saw them. I told them I was sorry they existed as a function to be ridden, or grown to be eaten. I left the show at the end of the season. I didn't ride a horse again for eighteen years.

I was not a mother, but I waited for a turn I had thought was coming ever since I was young. At twenty-five I was engaged to a man I thought I loved, and I bought two books about pregnancy, because my body told me it might be safe to have a child now. I felt my breasts and belly seem to soften and to bloom, as if they were enticing the acts that lead to a baby. I gained weight, I eased into a gentleness I had not let myself experience before, because I felt love and possibility. One day at the supermarket I bought a rattle in the baby supplies aisle. It was a wooden ring with plastic beads running on a groove through the centre of the circle. I bought a Tommee Tippee dummy, too, and carried them home, feeling them hot through my shoulder bag. I took my contraceptive pill faithfully but we talked about children, and I felt the shape of them just out of sight.

When the relationship ended, my imaginary children receded from the edges of my vision, and I let them go, passing the books on to friends who had children, recording their names and dates of birth on the inside covers. After each child was born the books came back to me a little more worn, the pages turned and marked with learning. I carted the books from flat to flat with all my other books. Some years, in some houses, I never even unpacked the box they were in, but I didn't forget about them. They burned in the box the way the rattle and the dummy did; dreams tucked away but still generating warmth.

I witness the birth of a friend's son, and it is the greatest day of my life. In the hospital everything runs smooth, and the hours sail by on greased wheels with barely a sound. I hold my friend's hand and stroke her forehead and I tell her to hang on when she sobs she's too tired. When the baby's head crowns I am gobsmacked. When his shoulders come through one by one, and his body slips from her like a small wet seal, I make sounds from the depth of me that are greetings, that are exaltations. I hold the light for the midwife to stitch up my friend. The metal and earth tang of blood is woven through the air. The boy latches to her breast and as the midwife stitches he feeds, and the world reassembles itself in a new order around his young life. I go out into a morning that has evolved from the midnight where we waited for him, and the sun on my skin is a baptism. I go home smiling. I cannot stop.

My mother taught all her children how to mother, first through the garden, then through the cats we adopted, and finally through the babies my sister and brother brought through. Her arms were the most comforting, and I saw her through the years as a shape in a quiet room, holding the children one by one, patting their backs in a slow rhythm, her head tucked against their tiny shoulders, breathing there. It was from her I learned how to hold the babies of my friends, how to wind them and lull them into sleep. I called her at midnight one evening when I was babysitting a child who would not stop crying, and she stayed on the phone with me until he was settled, instructing me in a steady voice to walk the living room, to pat his back. I said to her, 'I don't know how you did this for us every night, Mum.' She told me to wash my face and climb into bed.

Later I became a nanny. I found myself tangled in families of strangers, caring for children of all ages as if they were my own. I lived with a family of girls while their mother was away overseas. They did not have a father, and I took on the role of an extra parent in their mother's absence. It was difficult trying to navigate three girls on the edge of puberty. They ran hot with hormones and teenage despair, they were tricky, forgetful, deliberately unkind and confused. I called my mother the morning after the first night I stayed there, crying down the phone line, thanking her for everything she had done for me. She laughed, but I made a speech about how awful I must have been at that age and I forced her to hear that I understood now, that I was sorry. 'I had no idea,' I said. 'I just had no idea what you did for us.'

I have seen my mother almost every day of my life, but it took my dad's death to bring her into a focus that is hers alone. After his death we have more time. What she wants to do is see things grow, and with her I revert back to childhood, looking at plants with her, inspecting the old wooden troughs she has given to me, making sure they're in one piece and ready for new plants. I grow a salad and herb garden in the troughs she's had for several decades, and when the new growth comes through I am euphoric, because it grows in my history and in the history of my mother's hands. She comes to dinner, and I make salads from what I gather in the garden and I watch her eat and feel just like her. We go to a garden centre and cart wheelbarrows of flowers around the avenues where plants are stacked in aisles like a green Dewey decimal system. I lift the barrow and she walks beside me. I feel like her equal, and like her child, and I feel like a mother too, because I am watching out for her happiness. I am focused on her experience of life now Dad is gone. I am watching her grow, and develop new foliage and grow deeper roots in a life with less of him in it.

My mother joins an orchid society which meets

each month on Sundays to learn about the largest flower species in the world. Her house fills with orchids. The wardrobe has orchid plant feed on the shelves where the clothes should be. She sends me photographs of the plants she has cut back after their flowering is over for the year. She learns to use emojis and sends me sad faces because it's just shelves of plants with no flowers now for a good many months.

While she waits for the blooms to come back, she has a garden put in at the new house. The tractor-seat plants that line one wall of the little garden look like lily pads. She puts in stone pavers in an uneven line, and the plants we bought at the nursery grow between them, frothing green and travelling in every direction, leaving only hints about where you can step. Her grandchildren come to visit and hop from stone to stone, imagining they are in a fairy kingdom, or on the yellow brick road in Oz, and I see my mother smiling through the kitchen window, watching them do exactly as she had hoped.

Her garden grows up and grows lush and begins to look less ordered as the plants take over, making their own patterns that worship the sun. When I visit, my mother is sitting in her garden reading a book, a queen in her green kingdom, the sun hitting her face so that her sadness at the loss of her husband is briefly erased in light. We always go back to the land in our grief, I realise. At home when I was younger, my mother's entreaties to come out into the garden always accompanied my bouts of sadness. I barely ever went, though she'd try to coax me. Now at the first nudge of despair I go anywhere green, and I listen to the weather and feel at least a little calmer. It is not the same as my mother's garden, but it is something.

In the second Covid-19 lockdown I am housebound and listless. It feels as if the whole country, and especially Tāmaki Makaurau, is waiting for something. I pace the living room, waiting for a baby that does not come. I am desperate to grow things. All I want is to be the soil for a child, but the waiting yields nothing and I am inconsolable. Our house is small, and I feel shut in. We have no garden to speak of. There is a little arid patch of land out the back with an old clothesline under some trees, a slab of uneven concrete, and some kind of power hub concealed in a white tube right in the middle of the lawn. There is nowhere to sit, except on the rangy grass beside the concrete. The earth there is so packed, the spade head breaks off before it leaves a dent in the ground, so I have no choice but to grow plants in pots and troughs on our balcony, where the roots they put down hit the false earth of terracotta and wood, limiting their spread like the clipped wings of a bird. After a winter of grey and rain, the troughs are boggy, the plants too wet to grow. They are missing the rhythm of the real earth the way that I am. We dwindle and grow limp beside each other. I grieve for things I have never had.

My mother comes around one Saturday and takes charge of my grief and my worry. She rips out all the dying plants and inspects them like a forensic expert, identifying the problems with the soil and the sunlight. What I need is nutrients, she says. I have good soil but I could use a boost. She turns compost and sheep pellets into the soil of the pots and the troughs, and we plant tomatoes, lettuces, chillis and herbs. She buys pea straw and packs all the baby plants with the sweet-smelling hay like she's tucking them in at night, keeping them warm while we wait for the cold bursts of weather that blow from the south to give way to a warmer summer. I crouch beside her while she works, sweeping up the loose soil, watering the plants, and carrying away the lost causes. It takes her barely any time at all to transform the balcony into a place of calm and order, where all the growing things look optimistic in the sun that has come out while she is here. She has beads of sweat on her neck, just as I remember. She shows me how to pinch out the lateral shoots on the tomato plants, and how to tie their stems to stakes when they grow bigger. She pulls off her gardening gloves and packs away her fork and trowel, but not before I run my fingers over their handles, feeling the grain of the wood that has smoothed to silky softness from decades in her hands. I pour her a glass of wine, and we sit in the sunshine. She asks me if I feel any better. I squint in the light and tell her maybe I do. 'Watch these plants take off now,' she says. 'You watch how they'll shoot up now they have what they need.'

Stars

In the end, we try IVF.

On the morning I call our fertility doctor I've been woken by my alarm to find my body rigid, my head twisted to one side, my neck seized. My shoulders are up around my chin, and my spine feels splintered. I try to climb out of a dream in which I open drawers and cupboards, look behind bookshelves and in the fridge. I lift the pictures away from their hooks on the wall, I pull up the carpet. I don't know what I am looking for, but in the end I find a piece of paper that says

You have lost your joy, Michelle Langstone.

Our doctor is kind. She makes murmuring sounds of understanding and care, and I feel wrapped in a softness I have not allowed myself to feel for a long time. Shame quickens in my stomach as I realise that the way she carefully arranged her features all those months ago when we first met, when I told her we would not be doing IVF—that expression that I took for lack of caring—was her tucking away what she knew would be coming, at my age, given the things she knew about my body before I did. I cry a bit on the phone as I ask about the next step and what we should do. She explains the order of my life over the next few months and I try to breathe, to embrace the statistic she gives me—a 20 percent chance of a baby instead of just 5 percent. I hang up and climb into my husband's lap, and he holds me there for a while. We listen to the silence in the house, and I begin to let myself dream.

—

I always loved getting blood tests as a kid. Bold, I'd stare right at the needle as it pierced the vein on the inside of my elbow. The nurse would tell me to look away, but I'd watch the blood pool into the tube and not wince a bit. I like medical things. I like to know that there is someone in charge of me when I need it, and I like the silent streams of self-knowledge that my blood carries out of my body to another place where it can be translated. Now, the prospect of needles administered into my abdomen every night makes me excited. But of course there are delays. Of course the one month I want my period to come, it is eight days late. I think I am pregnant, am astonished, and then confused by the negative tests, which I perform for six days in succession. Surely this unusual delay can't be for nothing? It is for nothing, and when I bleed I am angry at my body for holding me up.

I go to collect the first lot of syringes and high-dose drugs from the fertility clinic. The woman in reception rummages through a pile of bags on the floor—there must be twenty of them there, for twenty women just like me. They look like the goody bags you get at a fashion show. She finds mine eventually and plonks the bag on the counter, where I pay her the largest amount of money I have ever put on my credit card. Outside, the winter air smacks my cheeks, and I can't stop smiling because I am finally doing something active and purposeful after months and months of witnessing my body do absolutely nothing. I put the syringes in the fridge door where the wine would usually go, and watch the clock for night time.

The first injection makes me feel nauseous. I had thought I would be able to administer it, but at the last minute I feel weak and ask Arun to do it. I turn the dial on the syringe cartridge, check and double-check the amounts, and hand it to him. I pinch the flesh and he stabs the needle in, and I don't feel anything but the pressure of his hand. When it is over, the nausea rises, swift like an ambush. I lie down and breathe, and imagine what is happening in my body now, with this rush of hormones circulating, greeting my reproductive organs with their special cocktail of altering substances like the dealer everyone waits for at a party.

Not a single forum in the world is any good when you are vulnerable. Even the ones created by successful survivors carry the ghosts of horror stories in their happy words. I am not on Facebook, so I can't join the IVF groups my friends have talked about, but I meander through the avenues of the internet looking for IVF forums against my better judgement. Everywhere, faceless women discuss their ages and their expectations, their fears and their losses. I have opened a Pandora's box of grief and hope and I can't look away, even as it drives me mad. There is a story about every conceivable aspect of IVF, and when I add the stories of these strangers to the stories of my friends I feel afraid. One woman has done eight rounds of IVF and is so obviously broken by it that the responders in the thread don't know what to say: trails of sad-faced emojis replace the words that wouldn't help her anyway. I collect these women's heartaches and joys the way that I collect the statistics for my age, lining up the percentages beside the losses and the wins, measuring myself alongside a yardstick of maternity that reaches across the whole world. I am stretched thin with the things I know. For every percentage of a statistic I am afforded, I see the deficit of the remaining numbers and how they stack against me.

I have an obsessive-compulsive need to know every single thing I can about IVF, and read medical journals from all over the world about supplements and therapeutic modalities and their impact. With my doctor's permission I order a hormone supplement not used in New Zealand, and begin to take it, spurred on by the medical papers and the test results. Even as I do this, as I prime my body with all the vitamins and minerals it probably already has, I understand I will never know if any of them have worked. Fertility is an imperfect science in which simple mathematical equations do not add up. I can do all these things, turn my life upside down in the pursuit of improving my egg health and my endometrial receptivity, but the specialists will never be able to pinpoint what I did that was successful if we do manage to have a baby. Still, I line up the tablets and the capsules and the sprays on the bench, and fill the two tall glasses of water needed to swallow all these things every day, and stare at the slip of paper Arun has stuck to the kitchen wall with Blu-Tack. It is a tiny note I left for him to find one day. I press my fingers to smooth the edges that have curled from the fug of steam from the stovetop, and read the words I left for him. *I love you.*

I love you, I tell my body. I love you, please work for me.

Days of needles into the flesh of my abdomen, leaving tiny bruises that float like little blue clouds around my belly button. I start to swell as my ovaries extend with eggs. I read somewhere that ovaries begin the size of grapes and, at the end of an IVF cycle, are as big as mandarins. At the scan that tracks the number of follicles I have grown, I hold my breath as the ultrasound wand moves inside me. A trainee technician peers at a screen, and she and her supervisor count what they can see. There are seven follicles of various sizes. They had told me that they would expect perhaps seven or eight follicles for a woman my age, but I am crushed. It does not feel like enough. No number would feel like enough, but less than double digits seems a blow. I go to get a blood test, and I stab at my husband with sharp words of anxiety. I push him, meting out my fear to wound him. It's not fair, but I do it, because I can't bear to be alone in the sense of hopelessness, in the absence of control. We drive home in silence. It is raining and I lean my head against the car window, watching the water streaming. I am worried that what I have done is not enough. All these months of health were not enough.

I walk up the maunga, increasing my pace so I am almost running, facing the winter cold with my mouth set in a tight line. I am terrified of the egg retrieval that is coming. I am afraid of the phone calls that will follow afterwards, where strangers from the clinic will tell me how many of my eggs have been fertilised, and how many make it to Day 3 and then to Day 5. Fear of the phone is an old phobia from when it brought bad news when I was young, and then again with Dad's prognosis. I can't wriggle out of the feeling of impending doom.

I read about fertilisation, and learn that when a sperm fertilises an egg there is a tiny flash of light, a little burst of energy—enough to turn the lights on. I watch a video, see a stranger's egg in a laboratory light up like a firefly or the twinkle of a far-off star. It is a magic I am unprepared for, and I can't stop thinking about when my eggs will meet my husband's sperm in the lab and light up in recognition. Nobody will be there to see them turn on. In the dark of the laboratory they will wink and glimmer in a cellular constellation. Some will fall dark and die, and others will survive until the next measurement. I can't get it out of my head that there will be nobody there to see them. They are away from home. I have traded the soft comfort of my ovaries for the sterility of test tubes, and the thought leaves me ragged with sadness.

I forget I have left my underwear on. I lie down in the hospital room to have my eggs retrieved, and the doctor has to ask me to take them off. Crimson, I wriggle them down my trembling legs and hand them to Arun, who puts them in his pocket, looking nonplussed. I sit back on the bed, lift my legs into the stirrups and lie down like an uncomfortable starfish.

When the drugs come I feel an ocean pour through

my veins, a warm flood of softness that lifts me away from the room. I can't see, but I hear Arun and the doctor chatting about television, while the nurse and lab technicians prepare to receive my eggs. I come in and out, yelping when the needle pierces the most quiet parts of my anatomy, and then I drift, my blood a boat I float in. I hear the embryologist counting as the individual eggs are passed through the window to her. One, two—Arun squeezes my hand and I come round to see his face hovering close to mine. Six, I hear, and then I slip away again.

When it's over I wobble back to the cubicle, drag on my undies and wrap up in my warm clothes. They make us wait, make me drink hot tea and eat Marmite on toast. The drugs leave my body, and the doctor sticks his head around the door to give us the final count. Fourteen. I ask him if he is sure, and he says he is, though they won't all be mature enough to fertilise. It's a good number, and he smiles and closes the door. I sob, and we are hustled back out into the day, clearing the cubicle of the traces of our hope, making way for the next woman. I go home and climb into bed, and the ache comes upon me, spreading through my womb, an iron warming up and pressing down. Mum comes round and sits beside me on the bed and asks what happens now. Now we wait, I say.

We have to wait a day to see which of the fourteen eggs will achieve fertilisation and become Day 1 blastocysts. I lie in bed through the afternoon, imagining them mingling with Arun's sperm, wondering which of our eggs and sperm will be wallflowers and which will be bold and go for it. I close my eyes and see the lights come on one by one. I am awake for some of every hour that night, checking the time, staring into the dark, imagining the lights.

When the sun comes up, I am relieved and bone-weary. Someone I love did IVF, and she got eighteen eggs in her first retrieval but only three fertilised. I can't think how I'll escape the same fate, because I am older than she is and the odds are stacked against me. I stalk the morning hours, waiting for the phone call from the lab, walking circuits of our tiny living room, checking my phone's volume again and again.

It goes like this: you wake six times in the night, every night, and when dawn comes you drag yourself up the maunga, filling in time until the next phone call. You never know when they will ring; it could be any time of day. You leave the volume on your phone up high and jump each time there's a text, feeling rage when someone who is not from the clinic calls you. Your nerves jangle, you can't eat, your hands shake. You have no control over anything that happens, or over the torrent of emotions that arrive at unpredictable moments.

On the third day, a crucial day, when you are waiting to hear how many of your eleven surviving blastocysts have made it to Day 3, you sob in the rain on your second trip up the maunga, at four in the afternoon. There has been no news. You imagine them all dead, the test tubes being rinsed in a basin and placed into a steriliser ready for the next devotion to attempted life. You play out the conversation at the clinic: your doctor demurs about being the one to call, and the nurses draw straws about who will make contact and give you the bad news. 'Michelle,' they will say—'is this a good time to talk? Could you give me your date of birth, please? Michelle, of your eleven blastocysts, none have made it to Day 3. I'm sorry. Have a rest and have a think, and then perhaps come in to see your doctor about what we can do next.' You can hear the words before they are said, and grieve for the end you know is coming.

In the rain, up Maungawhau, no birds are singing. You stand under open skies and let the water pound on the hood of your raincoat. You sniff the collar and it smells like a circus, and you remember the visit to the big top when you were a child, before they banned live animals. You watched greyhounds jump over spiked metal fences that got higher and higher as they cleared them, until the spikes almost touched the top of the tent and you expected to see those grey dogs impaled up there. The audience gasped and you wanted to scream for it to stop, but still they jumped, higher and higher, their bellies so soft and vulnerable above the metal. You hated that circus. You never went to a circus again after that.

The phone rings, but for a moment you don't notice, because you've changed the ringtone to the song of tūī and think the birds up the maunga have started singing again. You dash for the trees that line the road to the crater and shelter beneath them, the fat drips of water falling down the back of your neck because you've pulled your hood back to take the call. 'Ten of your eggs have made it to Day 3,' the nurse says. 'A very good number, but expect to see them drop away by Day 5,' she cautions. 'We always see them drop,' she says.

You hang up the phone and you can't even be happy about this news, because there are another two days to wait, and another round of news that may be bad. It is always like this—no chance to celebrate a milestone, because there is another to clear, and then another and another. Make it to Day 3; now make it to Day 5. Whoever survives to Day 5 gets tested for genetic soundness; whoever passes those tests can be transferred. Then you will wait to see if the embryo takes to your womb, and that will be ten days of agony and wondering. If your embryo embeds in your uterine lining and you are pregnant, you will take blood tests to watch if the hormones rise higher each day, and then you will wait for the seven-week scan, and then the twelve. It is never over. You walk home with your hood back, the rain all through your hair and your jersey and your trousers and your socks. You are just like those greyhounds, jumping for your life.

———

My embryos have cells taken from them, which will be sent to Christchurch, to a machine that can test for chromosomal abnormalities. The embryologist in charge of my blastocysts calls me on Day 5 to say they have nine embryos to test, and that he has very much enjoyed watching them grow, then gets off the phone to go and take the samples. When he calls me back, the tenth embryo he said was taking its time has caught up. Ten samples go to the South Island, where they wait for the samples from other women, until there are a hundred. The machine that does testing called Pre-implantation Genetic Screening is too expensive to run on less than a complete load, and so we wait for other women and I fall into another anxious spiral. It does not help that I read message boards. On one of them, a woman has sent eight embryos for PGS testing and none has come back to her.

Euploid, I learn, is the name for a healthy embryo. Aneuploid means destined to fail. I never wanted this, this superior selection—it seems counter-intuitive to bringing in life if you can tell one embryo it can come along for the ride, but not another. In the grading, my embryos are all excellent, but there is no way to tell just from looking who is normal and who is not. When I learn that about 80 percent of miscarriages in the first trimester occur because of abnormalities in the genetic make-up of the embryos, I begin to understand why it matters to test mine. At my age it is hoped there will be one, perhaps two euploid embryos. From a raft of ten, it seems like such a small number.

My anxiety deepens over the weeks we wait. I can take some comfort that at least my embryos are away from me, in cold sleep in a freezer, waiting too. I can't hurt them with my worry. A friend in Christchurch sends me weather reports to make me laugh. She says she hopes my embryos are enjoying Te Waipounamu. Even though they are only cells, not whole embryos, it pleases me to think they are on vacation and seeing some sights while they await examination. I imagine them being taken for a punt on the Avon, and realise I am exhausted.

When our doctor calls weeks later, it is on a Sunday, and we are driving to Arun's grandad's funeral. When I hear her voice down the line, I go cold. I do not want bad news on this day. She says we have three viable embryos, and talks about a few things to do with transferring them. I have stopped listening because I am imagining the seven miscarriages I might have had before reaching one of my good three if we hadn't done the testing. I feel appalled and grateful and worried all at once, but for the first time our doctor sounds optimistic, and it throws me. Three seems so few, but they are excellent embryos, she says, the best we could hope for.

I get off the phone, and we go to the funeral, where we lay roses and puffed rice in Bapa's coffin, and water from the river Ganga is poured into his mouth as a blessing. I go with Arun to the crematorium to say goodbye and watch the fire whoosh and engulf the flowers on top of Bapa's coffin, and feel grief for what is lost.

I get to know the phlebotomist at my local blood lab very well. His name is Sonu, and he used to be a train driver until he retrained a few years ago. He is always kind to me, taking my form and wishing me good morning when I see him. His needles never hurt, and he makes me laugh when he tells me that about 80 percent of the people who are scared of needles are men, and very often they are the same people who have tattoos and look tough. He tells me about his sister-in-law who has gone through IVF, encourages me to keep going, to ask questions, to push for good communication with my clinic. He comforts me the first time our embryo transfer is cancelled because my hormone surge has been missed. A computer program has collected my data and decided when I should start testing my blood for the luteinising hormone that indicates ovulation is coming, but I go off-piste in my cycle and the transfer can't go ahead. Now there is another month to wait.

I cry so hard I scare my cat. Even though it is only a month, and we still have our embryos, to fall at this last hurdle seems unforgivable and unnecessary, especially when I find out that I could have tested from Day 7, instead of Day 10, and not missed the chance at all. I lay out in no uncertain terms to the nurses at the clinic that I am not prepared to go through this again, that I am happy to test from Day 7, even if it means a week or more of daily blood tests.

I say goodbye to Sonu, tell him I'll see him in another month, and he pats me on the shoulder and says he will be waiting.

Every morning at seven I am waiting at the door of the clinic. I am never first in line—there are always others there. I try to guess what they're being tested for, but the only ones I'm certain about are the women clutching yellow forms. These are the forms for fertility, and ensure we get tested as soon as possible so our blood can be sent off by courier before 9 a.m. Some days we smile at each other in the waiting room; other days we stare at our forms or at the walls.

Today I am shuffled into Room 3, which is Sonu's room, and he takes my blood and tells me this time the transfer will happen. We repeat the test for eight days in a row, by which time I am a husk of exhaustion. But the blood tests show the surge, and things begin to move.

I go to get a scan, and the nurses peer at the screen, measuring the thickness of my uterine lining, making murmuring noises of approval. I could kiss the nurse who tells me my lining is wonderful and that my body is doing exactly what it should for me. I fly out of the clinic with my date confirmed for the transfer.

I forget my tiredness and go walking, feeling the spring sun on my nose and forehead. I stop to buy an ice cream and stand in the shade beside the dairy to eat it, feeling lucky.

I begin to miss my embryos. In the night I can't sleep, and I place my hands over my belly and imagine they are back in there where they belong. I feel how far away from me they are, those three tiny pieces of us, and I ache to have them back in my body. I do not like having my DNA elsewhere. I imagine what will happen if there is a power cut at the clinic and the emergency generators turn on to keep the freezers cool. What if the generators stop working? I get up and ease open the sliding door to the balcony and stand in the cold air, and the cat comes to nose around my legs, thrilled by this night outing. I can feel the fear coming again. The shadows of all the stories of other women and their IVF journeys attach themselves to my body like wraiths, keeping me down in the dark with my fear and the ghosts of lost babies.

I go to see a hypnotherapist who specialises in fertility, because I want to see if I can shift the fear, or at least make it my pet. In her little room which is a nest of couches and soft blankets and paperwork, she teaches me how to tap on my meridian lines, to soften my anxiety, and how to visualise my embryos and wrap them in light and love. Then she puts me under. I slip through my consciousness like I am weighted down. I hear her ask me to imagine a safe place, and I find myself at the bottom of the sea, in a water bed, the sheets pulled up to my chin as a shoal of fish darts silver above me. An octopus makes its way across to see me, kicking up sand behind him as he comes, and I wave at him. In this state I don't register embarrassment at the strangeness of my safe place where, if logic prevailed, I would swiftly drown. I experience only a sense of wonder as I watch a pod of dolphins turn this way and that above me. It all seems perfectly normal to be in a bed on the ocean floor, smiling at cephalopods.

The therapist asks me to transport myself into my womb now, and to feel the warmth and shape of it. I stand in there, and it feels crowded and soft. She tells me to decorate the space for the arriving embryo, and without thinking I bring in the wool blanket that my parents gave me, and a basket of books, and a painting of flowers, even though I'm sure it's warm enough in there and I know the baby can't read yet. The flowers are wisteria, and I realise I am decorating my womb like my childhood bedroom, where the flowers hung outside my window and I'd wake to the buzz and the tap of bumblebees on the glass. The therapist introduces a guardian who she says is looking after my womb, and whose job it is to welcome the embryo when it is transferred. I sit beside the being on the little bed I have made, and in the golden light her outline reminds me of Massey, my adopted grandmother. Peace comes over me like a drug, and I sleep in there, with her hand resting on my leg just like it used to when I was a child. When the therapist draws me out of the hypnotic state, I am staggered to see half an hour has gone by. It has felt like seconds.

We tell ourselves we don't believe in signs, but my sister and I always look for them. We looked for four-leaf clovers when we were smaller, poring over the lawn grass, deciding if we found one it would mean something specific, like we could go to Disneyland, or a letter would come in the mail from Dad—one he'd told us to look out for while he was overseas. Later, and especially after Dad died, we looked for the significance of dates and times as signs, of birds arriving when we were thinking of him, or rainbows or fog when we didn't expect it. I come to think of gannets as my dad sending a message, because they always appear when I least expect it and when he is on my mind.

The luck of birds is something we have believed in since childhood, from when we retrieved nests after storms, and rescued eggs and baby birds, and tried to hatch or raise them. We two were obsessed with birds' eggs and the tidy precision of nests. We had a book called *Ratsmagic*, in which a bluebird is kidnapped by a witch, right when she is due to lay her egg. The animals in the valley where she lives whisper to one another, '*Bluebird is with egg, BLUEBIRD IS WITH EGG*' with fierce importance. The laying of the egg will set the course of destiny in the story. It was a dark tale, and beautiful. *Bluebird is with egg*, we'd whisper to each other in the dark of our bedroom at night. *Bluebird is with egg*, we'd say at the bathroom sink, our mouths full of toothpaste. Years later, when my sister became pregnant with her daughter, I was the first person she told. A message came in the early afternoon of a dark winter's day that read simply: *Bluebird is with egg.* She called her first-born daughter Ava. 'Like a bird,' she told me when I went to visit her at Birthcare—her name means 'like a bird'.

On the morning of my embryo transfer I take myself up the maunga to get the blood flowing around my body, hoping it will help the receptivity of my womb. I walk fast and I listen to the tūī puncturing the air with their joyful trills and whistles, and I hear the industry of their wings. On the way home a little curve of white on the concrete catches my eye. I pass by it, then double back to look. It is the perfect snow-white half of a pigeon's egg, and the other half nests inside it. There is no fluid and no feather inside the shell, so I know it is the remnants of a fully hatched bird, now out in the world and free. I hold it in my hand and feel its lightness and possibility, admire the thin, luminous shell that has split to make way for life. I place it out of harm's way and carry on.

—

I know by now not to expect sensitivity and beauty in the processes we go through in IVF. It is a carousel of function and statistics and facts—there is no room for romance and the Pollyanna parts of my nature. I have to make do on my own, packing a chunk of rose quartz into my handbag to take to the clinic on the morning of our transfer, persuading Arun to lie with me and visualise our embryo, surrounding it with light and love the way I have been taught, letting it know it is coming home now.

At the clinic I am shepherded into a cubicle, and handed a gown and a piece of paper with information on follow-up care. I remember to take my undies off, and fold them carefully beside my jeans, placing my jersey on top so nobody can see them. I sit in a chair opposite Arun, who has gone very still and silent. I ask him what the matter is, and he tells me he is excited, but I think he is scared. We check my details with a nurse and trot down the hall to the theatre we were in last time, where two embryologists peer at us through a little window in the wall, safe in their lab with my embryo. The doctor is a new one to me. She has the fast energy of a runner, and goes through my details for a second time, her voice both energised and perfunctory. Her eyebrows are like busy creatures darting across her forehead as she listens to my questions. The embryologists tell me the embryo they have chosen has thawed well and is ready to go. It has fully hatched from its shell and is ready to implant, they say. In the far corner of the room is a computer, and a photo comes up there of my embryo. It looks like a telescopic photo of a star, with an uneven surface and a faint halo of purple around it.

I hoist my legs up into the stirrups in a move that now feels practised, while the nurse and doctor unpeel the plastic around the sterilised instruments. Cold gel is squeezed onto my stomach, and the ultrasound wand presses in deep to find the image of my womb. I have drunk three glasses of water to make sure my bladder is full, allowing them to see my insides better, and I wince, worried I will wet myself, as the nurse presses. The doctor says she hopes I like the music and I realise the radio is playing Madonna's 'Crazy For You'. I sing along with her in my head, and see myself dancing in the rumpus room with my sister.

Arun squeezes my hand tight while the cold implements go in and open up the passageway into the heart of me. It hurts, and I breathe deep and slow, fixed on the ceiling and the song. They have to clamp back parts of me to get in at the right angle, and I endure it, and try to stay calm, thinking only of the embryo. When they have everything in position, the doctor tells me that the embryologist will now 'walk my embryo through', and I turn my head to see the door to the lab opening, an assistant holding it back for the person carrying my embryo to enter the room. She is walking with immense care, like a bridesmaid, I think—step together, step together. I decide it must be because she doesn't want to trip and drop the syringe, but it's very formal, and the room takes on an odd feeling, as if we are in a performance, all taking our choreographed positions while Madonna sings.

The doctor and embryologist crouch so they are at eye level with my insides, and all I can see are the tops of their heads, and the wiggling eyebrows of the doctor as she frowns and instructs. The song on the radio changes and I think I have imagined it, then know I haven't, as the opening notes of guitar and then piano swell into ABBA's 'Chiquitita'. I get the giggles and try to repress it, my whole torso shaking with mirth and the ridiculous position of my body and the surreal moment I am in. The doctor says she is now walking the embryo into my womb. 'Tell it good luck,' she says. 'Good luck,' we say in unison. 'Welcome home,' I whisper under my breath. They watch the monitor for the little flash of light that shows them the air bubble holding my embryo has come through the tube and passed into me.

Piece by piece they remove the implements, handing them through the window to be checked under a microscope in case my embryo has gone rogue and attached itself to one of them. When the all-clear comes, they swivel the monitor to show me my murky insides and the tiny bubble they say houses my embryo. To me it is a lighter dab of grey in the darkness, but I stare hard at it, trying to send my love there. Everyone is packing up and getting ready for the next woman, whisking up the sheet, straightening the stirrups. I thank them as if I'm the last guest who has stayed too long at a party, and hurry out of the room. When I am changed we say goodbye to the nurse, who tells us she will email a photo of our embryo, and reminds us that our blood test to check if I'm pregnant is in ten days' time. Outside the cars go too fast, and I squint in the sunshine, confused by the speed at which things happened, dazzled by the knowledge of life inside. I kiss my husband goodbye and go home, and watch stand-up comedy clips one after another because I have heard laughter is good for implantation.

—

I sleep with the photo of the embryo under my pillow. I roll over in the night and hear its papery whisper as it moves against the sheet. The nights crawl, but not as much as the days, when I sit down to work and find myself staring out the window at things that do not even register. In this stasis I can barely think, but I examine my body for signs, checking and double-checking the internet for indications of pregnancy. It is no different from all the other times I tried to get pregnant on my own—I think I feel implantation pains, think my breasts swell, think the flush of nausea is upon me—but this time I know there is a viable embryo inside me, and there is a real chance it could survive and become my baby. I wish my belly was the hull of a glass-bottom boat, so I could watch events as they unfold in real time, in the obscure landscape of my womb.

We get through nine days of waiting until I can't stand it anymore and decide to take a home pregnancy test. On all the forums women say you can test from Day 7 after embryo transfer, and I decide I might as well, so at least I can be composed when the phone call comes on Day 10 with the news of success or failure. Today is my dad's birthday, and I'm looking for a sign—some good news, or a distraction from the reminder of the loss of him. I rouse Arun in the pitch black, and draw back the curtain in our bedroom so we can watch the lightening sky. My hands shake as I unwrap the test in the bathroom. I take it back to bed with me and curl up, and we listen to the birds singing the dawn in as the minutes count down. Happy birthday, Dad, I think. I never asked him the story of his birth, and I regret that, but I doubt he ever knew—arriving into a world of a practical and rigorous mother who had work to get on with, her boy with his sweet smile the last of six to leave her womb. On my birthday, Dad liked telling me how much trouble I'd caused coming in, and how that set the tone for the trouble I caused all through my life. I always let myself be teased, but I'd search my mother's face while he said it. She just smiled and said it wasn't an amazing birth but it was worth it. I recite the story to myself while I watch the seconds run out on my lit-up phone, watch the clouds loosen to reveal the morning star still visible in the lifted light.

My father held me close for the first few hours of my life and he didn't let go. My birth interrupted the evening news and the wellbeing of my mother, who bled on like a river, like a ribbon, like a tide around us, while the doctor pressed on her to staunch the flow and nurses came to help him. Dad was worried, but told my mother he would look after me, watching as they took her away for mending. He kissed my forehead and my closed eyes, he kissed my ears and the slick of blonde hair on my head, and he kissed my full, round cheeks. He drew me closer and told me that he loved me, and together we waited for my mother to return. The soft evening light came in through the curtains to wait with us.

In memory of

Dawson Langstone
28 *October* 1946 – 7 *December* 2018

Acknowledgements

This book is in the world because Michelle Hurley and Allen & Unwin took a chance on me—thank you, I am grateful for the opportunity. I was extremely fortunate to have Jane Parkin edit this book, and it was a privilege to work alongside her. Naomi Arnold was the first reader on several of these essays, and her clarity and friendship during uncertain times was a gift. I am so thankful for the encouragement of Jo Wane and Virginia Larson, who gave my writing a home at *North & South* magazine and set me on a new path. Thank you to Mark Broatch, who commissioned my very first piece of work and without whom I might not be writing at all, though he would say that's nonsense. (It isn't.) Lastly, I would not have been able to write this book if my husband Arun hadn't been there, calmly sorting through my other work with his beautiful clean eye, while I flapped around like an oversized hen, littering the house with anxious feathers. Thank you, Arun, you are the best.

Author photograph by Dean O'Gorman

About the author

Michelle Langstone is a well-known actor in both New Zealand and Australia, and has featured in multiple film and television roles, including recurring roles in *One Lane Bridge*, *800 Words* and *McLeod's Daughters*.

Michelle won the award for Best First Person Essay at the Voyager Media Awards in 2019 and the award for Best Interview or Profile at the Voyager Media Awards in 2020. She has written for *North & South* magazine, *New Zealand Listener*, *The New Zealand Herald* and The Spinoff website.